LÉON HATOT

© 2004 Assouline Publishing for the present edition
601 West 26th Street, 18th floor
New York, NY 10001, USA
Tel.: 212 989-6810   Fax: 212 647-0005
www.assouline.com
Texts © Léon Hatot

First published by Editions Assouline, Paris, France.

Translated from the French by Sandra Petch.

Color separation: Gravor (Switzerland)
Printed by **Partenaires-Livres**® (JL)

ISBN: 2 84323 471 9

LÉON HATOT

ARLETTE E. EMCH

ASSOULINE

Bienne December 17th, 2004

Léon Hatot, one of the great artists in jewelry and European culture was a worthy candidate for a book about himself and his work.

It is now done. Arlette E. Emch who brings him back to life has researched with care and written with passion and emotion about the life and work of this exceptional man.

I wish you much pleasure reading this book.

Sincerely yours

Nicolas G. Hayek
Chairman and cofounder of the Swatch Group Ltd

Foreword

The thousands of sketches of watches, jewelry, fashion and luxury accessories devised and penned by the master jeweler Léon Hatot over the first third of the twentieth century testify to his immense talent. It is this inestimable trove almost entirely dedicated to women, that the Swatch Group acquired in 1999.

At present its only all-jewelry brand, Léon Hatot reinforces the Swatch Group's presence in the magical and exclusive world of luxury. Fashioned in the crucible of inventiveness that was Art Deco, its historic and artistic legacy remains a prized source of beauty and supreme elegance, leavened by treasures of imagination, creativity, technical virtuosity and expert craftsmanship.

Each of the thousands of drawings that had been locked away in a vault since the Second World War remains a source of inspiration for the designers, jewelers and watchmakers working for the Léon Hatot company today. Their mission is to draw inspiration from the Léon Hatot spirit and learn to interpret his unique approach before giving contemporary form to a creative process steeped in the styles of the madcap Roaring Twenties and Art Deco's aesthetic discipline.

Alongside constantly renewed collections, designs made in limited and individually numbered editions of manifest exclusivity are sold in Léon Hatot's own boutiques and at topflight jewelers around the world.

2005 marks the one-hundredth anniversary of the brand. In 1928 Léon Hatot had moved his business to premises on Rue du Faubourg Saint-Honoré, an area favored by the cream of Parisian society. Equally taken by his creations were prestigious Place Vendôme jewelers, since Léon Hatot's skill and talent were sought out by many of his colleagues and competitors, as his company's storied production registers show.

It took the expertise and know-how of the world's leading watch manufacturer to make the most of this fabulous treasure. It takes the courage and professional resources of a dedicated team to bring it to the public's attention. And it will take the beauty of womanhood to bring it back to life.

the man who would give impetus and originality to the
measurement and artistic expression of time was born in
April 1883, in the unassuming Burgundy town of
Châtillon-sur-Seine. Barely twelve years later, Léon Hatot joined
the students at the Besançon school of watchmaking, continuing
his education after 1898 at the city's school of fine arts. At one he
learned the technician's precision while at the other he developed
his artistic flair. The future would prove him right to have thus
nurtured his natural dispositions for rigor and fantasy, both
equally important in his chosen field.

Léon Hatot was just twenty-two when, unafraid to take risks, he
made clear his determination to be independent and set up his
own business in the city that had taught him his trade. Soon a

dozen craftsmen were employed at what would rapidly become the company's specialties of jewelry-making, engraving precious metals, and the assembly and finishing of exceptional watches.

With each passing day, Hatot learned the subtleties of his profession. Meanwhile, the world was seduced by the extravagant new lifestyle that was flourishing in the Paris of the Belle Époque.

At this turn-of-the-century, all around the world colossal fortunes, both new and old, were growing apace… more often than not to be spent in Paris. Fashion and its train of accessories inspired ever more audacious, even avant-garde creations while fashionable society engaged in an endless array of gastronomic delights and pastimes in establishments whose name and reputation traveled to the four corners of the globe. Paris was the city everyone wanted to see… if only to be seen there themselves. Who could resist the siren's call of a capital that had become the scintillating City of Light?

For Léon Hatot, the opportunity came in early 1911. Without hesitation he seized his chance and became the new owner of Brédillard, an established Parisian supplier to the leading names in luxury watches and jewelry, the very ones that courted their customers on Rue de la Paix and Place Vendôme. Already a specialist in jewelry watches, the young entrepreneur now disposed of the ideal means with which to embark on his own conquest of Paris, and with it the world.

It wasn't long before his name emblazoned the delivery slips for the sumptuous jewelry watches that would adorn the wrists of Parisian society. He fitted them with the finest movements available, many of which were finished and assembled in the Hatot workshop in Besançon. His customers, all prestigious names, were quick to acknowledge that here was a force to be reckoned with, a man whose models superbly captured the prevailing mood. At a time when the Art Nouveau style was still very much in vogue, Léon Hatot found inspiration in eighteenth-century motifs, in particular the laurel branches, garlands and delicate patterns of the Louis XVI style. He forged a reputation that soon imprinted itself on everyone's mind, even convincing the political authorities of his talent. The City of Besançon, for example, commissioned him to create the elegant hunter watch that was presented to President Armand Fallières to commemorate his official visit to the region.

When war broke out in 1914, Hatot was enlisted. Here was an opportunity for him to use his technical skills for his country. And so he distinguished himself with the invention of a cost-effective process to manufacture mechanical artillery parts.

With peace came a new era when women were at last relieved of the burden of tradition that had weighed on their lives and social status. Although they were not immediately granted the political rights to which they aspired, these still being reserved for men, in all domains women now enjoyed far greater freedom of movement, in every sense of the term. As men had been called to arms, thousands of women had answered present to take their place in factories and offices where comfort and safety had dictated a new style of dress. Gone were the heavy draped outfits of the pre-war years, replaced by lightweight dresses in easy-to-wear cuts. In a shocking provocation, intricate chignons and bouffant coiffures disappeared as women bobbed and cropped their hair. Corsets were hung up and forgotten; out went ruffles and frills and in came the delightful cloche hat. Jewelry, as much a part of any outfit as clothes or hairstyle, underwent its own transformation.

By 1919 Léon Hatot had resumed production of luxury watches, buoyed by the post-war period's new-found freedoms, in particular by an artistic current whose early stirrings predated the war. Called Art Deco, it took its name from the famed International Exhibition of Modern Decorative and Industrial Arts held in Paris in 1925.

In jewelry, the wristwatch held center-stage throughout the "fast and furious" Twenties, its metamorphosis spurred on by the new sleeveless fashions that drew attention to ladies' bare arms. Constantly on show, the wristwatch evolved from a purely functional object to an accessory that reflected the personality and taste of its wearer, and which women were quick to adopt. For Léon Hatot, here was an opportunity to express the full extent of his talent. He miniaturized the movement which he housed inside a slim case; he also concealed the dial behind a cover which became his canvas, enhancing it with a constellation of precious stones and other luxurious materials that soon spilled over onto the strap, originally in moiré. Soon the precious wristwatch rivaled with jewelry as the finishing touch to elegant evening wear.

When designing his watches, Léon Hatot favored vertical compositions in harmony with the long and slender shape of the new feminine silhouette. Time was given on an often rectangular dial paired with a similarly shaped case whose streamlined form recalled the bodywork of the fabulous cars that sped up and down Parisian boulevards, or the fuselage of the planes now conquering the sky.

The modern world and city life, two leitmotivs of the Futurist movement, in turn inspired Hatot. He experimented with new cuts for precious stones, creating unprecedented play on light. He dreamed up geometric patterns to adorn a wrist, neck or waist, with ingenious inlays of white upon white in which diamonds dazzled against platinum. Sometimes, for the pleasure of contrast, he would juxtapose opaque stones such as onyx, coral or jade. Flouting the rules of materials that should and shouldn't mix, Hatot conceived astonishing combinations of colors and shapes that echoed the art of the Fauvists and Cubists in their quest to push back the boundaries of painting.

Decoration, furniture and architecture were infused with the same reviviscence that reached its pinnacle in the flamboyant Ballets Russes. With each new season, *le Tout-Paris* would flock, heart racing, to experience the explosion of sound, movement and color orchestrated by Serge Diaghilev. Music, dance, painting, theatre and fashion came together as never before in this talented magician's hands.

For Léon Hatot, such modernity not only swept artistic creation; it embraced technology too.

When the trade magazine *La France Horlogère* invited him to join its editorial committee, he was introduced to readers as an "industrialist and artist". Indeed, as inventive as ever, alongside his jewelry creations Léon Hatot had long since turned his thoughts to ways of applying electrical energy, now "transportable", to watchmaking.

as early as 1920 he set up a subsidiary tasked with researching and developing battery-driven timepieces. Three years later, under the "ATO" brand, Hatot launched a range of electrical clocks that were manufactured in his Besançon workshops. They blended perfectly with contemporary furniture, itself inspired by the pared-down aesthetics of the Bauhaus movement. Some were finished with precious woods, marble or chromed metal while others were encased in a pressed glass frame, made by the Lalique crystal company. Hatot's clocks enjoyed an immediate success that the Universal Exhibition of 1925 would confirm.

The French jewelry section inside the Grand Palais went down as one of the highlights of this unprecedented event. Exhibition rules stipulated that "only genuinely original works of new inspiration" would be accepted, and that "copies and imitations of existing styles" would be systematically refused. Léon Hatot showed his revolutionary clocks and supremely feminine wristwatches. Their success was rewarded with a Grand Prix, an amply deserved tribute to such inventiveness and extreme elegance. Further distinction came when Léon Hatot was made a Knight of the Legion of Honor.

The post-war scramble for luxury and pleasure continued. Europe was determined to put the past behind it and, driven by an overwhelming lust for life, set about creating a new world. Its hopes would be dashed by a certain Black Thursday in late 1929.

Paris was drunk on pleasure. The city developed a passion for the movies and was caught up in the wave of unprecedented sounds and rhythms called jazz. The Parisians learned to dance the Charleston and, thanks to the *Revue Nègre* and Josephine Baker, the ebony goddess who reigned over Paris nights, discovered an exoticism and sensuality they had never before known. Excited crowds would gather ringside while others set sail for the New World aboard imposing ocean liners.

The flapper threw herself headlong into this whirlwind of freedom. She discovered sport and the fun of outdoor pursuits, daring to bare her skin to the sun's warmth. She took to smoking, exhibiting extravagant cigarette cases and holders and would take out her compact in public to reapply kohl and coral to lids and lips.

Giving free rein to his imagination, Léon Hatot designed and created innumerable accessories to complement her elegance. His coveted creations reflected the general relaxing of attitudes and the emergence of infinitely more varied and daring pleasures. His *nécessaires* accompanied ladies through the night and into dawn, cleverly combining in the least possible space a mirror, a compact, a lipstick holder, a comb, a cigarette case and lighter, and sometimes even a miniature watch.

The Orient, which fascinated western craftsmen and artists, held a wealth of ideas for Léon Hatot. The unique sense of space in Japanese art, along with the patterns, colors and materials it employed in its creations, inspired him for many of his watches, jewelry and accessories. Hatot's jewelry and luxury watch assembly workshops enjoyed growing success. In 1926 he placed his son-in-law Édouard Dietsch at their helm. He would prove a gifted second-in-command as he further developed the firm's specialties of watches and jewelry, both of which continued to captivate lovers of exceptional creations.

In 1928 Léon Hatot transferred his activities to luxurious premises at 12, Rue du Faubourg Saint-Honoré. From here he could directly welcome the cosmopolitan clientele who, while never any less demanding, remained fascinated by the proliferation and quality of his creations.

In the late nineteen-twenties, Hatot turned his attention to a new challenge: to perfect a watch with a simple and reliable self-winding movement. In 1930 he received the first in a series of patents that acknowledged him as the creator of a self-winding mechanism that has remained virtually unchanged to this day. The entire movement moved back and forth in a frame, supported by tiny ball bearings that regulated its rate. Hatot named his invention the "Rolls", adapting it to match the small size of the rectangular ladies' watches that were particularly in vogue at that time.

To quote Joan Crawford's elegant definition, "The watch Rolls is eternity in a box."

When war broke out again in 1939, the entire stock of Léon Hatot's workshop was locked in a bank vault for safekeeping. When fifty years later this exceptional assortment of watches and jewelry came under the hammer it created quite a stir.

The collection was sufficiently important to warrant a special sale at Christie's Geneva. This took place on May 10th 1989 in the prestigious setting of the Hotel Richemond, decorated for the occasion with panels relating the history and art of this master jeweler.

The auction, a unique opportunity to acquire original pieces complete with a copy of their stock slip, aroused extensive interest as much among collectors and traders as lovers of fine watches. They bid eagerly for the different movements and even for unfinished pieces.

The sale was presided, with brio, by François Curiel, Chairman of Christie's Europe. In the space of two thrilling hours, with standing room only from start to finish, each lot found a taker. At the end of the day the announcement came that sales had more than tripled estimates.

The combination of the Hatot name, the guarantee of extraordinary beauty and technicity, the Art Deco style, and the perfect condition of watches and jewelry which for the most part had never been worn, meant that each lot commanded a sensational price.

o be a woman... something these leading lights of the first third of the twentieth century never forgot. Beautiful, liberated, bold, sensual, intelligent trailblazers, they lit up the nights and enchanted the days of their contemporaries. Their legacy lives on, brought to us by that remarkable observer of his times, Léon Hatot. He had the eye to decipher their lifestyle, to interpret their desire to seduce. He gave wings to their beauty, their sensuality, their new-found freedom. For them he created parures that were inspired by the era and its succession of aptly-named moods: the Belle Époque, the Roaring Twenties, Art Nouveau and Art Deco.

For this was an era of art and abandon, beauty and extravagance. It was also when Léon Hatot discovered Van Gogh, Gauguin, Cézanne, Matisse, Picasso, Modigliani and the Ballets Russes. This surge of creative energy could but influence his own ideas, jewelry, watches and parures. All are intimate objects, worn against the skin and which speak volumes about the personality of the women they adorn.

Seven women among others left their mark on this overture to the twentieth century. They were Amy Johnson, Louise Brooks, Isadora Duncan, Josephine Baker, Lina Cavalieri, Renée Perle and Elsa, the beautiful stranger.

Seven remarkable women leading seven very different lives. And yet all were driven by an all-consuming quest for excellence and an extraordinary lust for life, tinged with an aura of mystery.

2005. A hundred years have gone by. *Éternel féminin...* always the same vitality, the same striving for excellence, the same revolutionary spirit. The pioneer is still a pioneer. The airwoman is now an astronaut too, the soprano a diva, the muse a symbol, the dancer an athlete, and the beautiful stranger a beautiful stranger. 2005. Proud of its fabulous heritage and intimately inspired by some five thousand original drawings, Léon Hatot master jeweler continues to address these women in a spirit that is as contemporary and as visionary as ever. No doubt as Léon Hatot would have wanted it to be, and as any art form demands.

Modern yes, though never turning its back on its origins. On the contrary. Léon Hatot plunges into its past to inspire its creativity. Its founder's spirit is never far away.

First of all, the number 7. Alongside one-off creations, haute couture and bespoke collections, certain jewelry and watch decors are so technically complex, or the stones that adorn them so rare, that only seven can exist. In the same spirit of excellence and originality, 77 is the number of pieces in a limited edition, worn by only a confidential circle.

Léon Hatot's spirit can also be felt in the collections and their enigmatic names. They bear the hallmark of a creativity and inventiveness to match that of the Roaring Twenties.

Sharp, linear, geometric, architectural Zelia. Amy Johnson could so easily have worn this collection's supple rings, transformable pendants, and watches that metamorphose from day to night. This pioneering Queen of the Air was also a true beauty.

Louise Brooks could have danced the Charleston, with her trademark black bob and the cabochon sapphires of the Aimay line fastened around her arm, coiled around her neck, and hung from her ears.

Barefoot, evanescent, floating, subtle, vertiginous: the Vertige collection looks to Isadora Duncan and to the free expression that is dance.

Luela. Who else but the ebony goddess Josephine Baker could inspire this line? Daring, exotic, unconventional, she was the first woman to appear almost naked on stage. Her image is inscribed in our memory.

Each new era brings its beauties, one of whom stands out as the most beautiful of all. Lina Cavalieri, the Italian diva, ranks among them. The enchantment of Éclat du Soir is made for her.

Countless women around the world know what it is to have their image immortalized again and again with talent and with love. Yet what is common today was once the exception. Superb Renée Perle, captured on film by Jacques-Henri Lartigue in a pose so contemporary as to become the creative impetus for the Kimay line.

And finally, the beautiful stranger. She is you and I. She is all the women to whom Léon Hatot dedicates Les Ailes du Désir.

again the spirit, the expertise and the exactingness of Léon Hatot... The finest metals, gold, platinum and steel. The most precious stones and gems – diamonds, sapphires, emeralds and rubies along with pearls. The most unusual stones: brazilianites, andalusites, azurites and fire opals. The rarest too, such as Paraiba tourmalines and Padparadscha sapphires. As well as the most appetizing, not least mandarin garnets. Each one is sought out with passion, selected with love, and recognized by the foremost experts.

Mystery is the key to Léon Hatot's timepieces. Like clothes that are designed to be worn from morning until night, with one ingenious movement a Léon Hatot watch opens in the daytime to display the hour. Then closes at night to become a jewel. A discreet companion, time keeps its secret. Zelia, Kimay, Vertige, Éventail, Éclat du Soir, Les Ailes du Désir, La Beauté du Diable, Nuage, Pompon: with every Léon Hatot watch, time retains its mystery.

The spirit of Léon Hatot appears again in the craftsmanship that is now synonymous with luxury, refinement, rarity, authenticity and perfection. Handmade. Each stone set by hand. The excellence of master craftsmen who perpetuate the finest Swiss traditions.

Each Léon Hatot creation is enhanced with an exclusive Coup de Foudre® diamond. It is cut to reveal, depending on the angle from which it is seen, eight arrows or eight hearts. It is the promise of quality and originality, a symbol of confidence and a discreet signature that gives Léon Hatot watches and jewelry their unique value.

And so the nostalgia of carefree days when the hours simply drifted by. A time when the light bathed everything in beauty. A time of giddy freedom, of rhythms and colors…

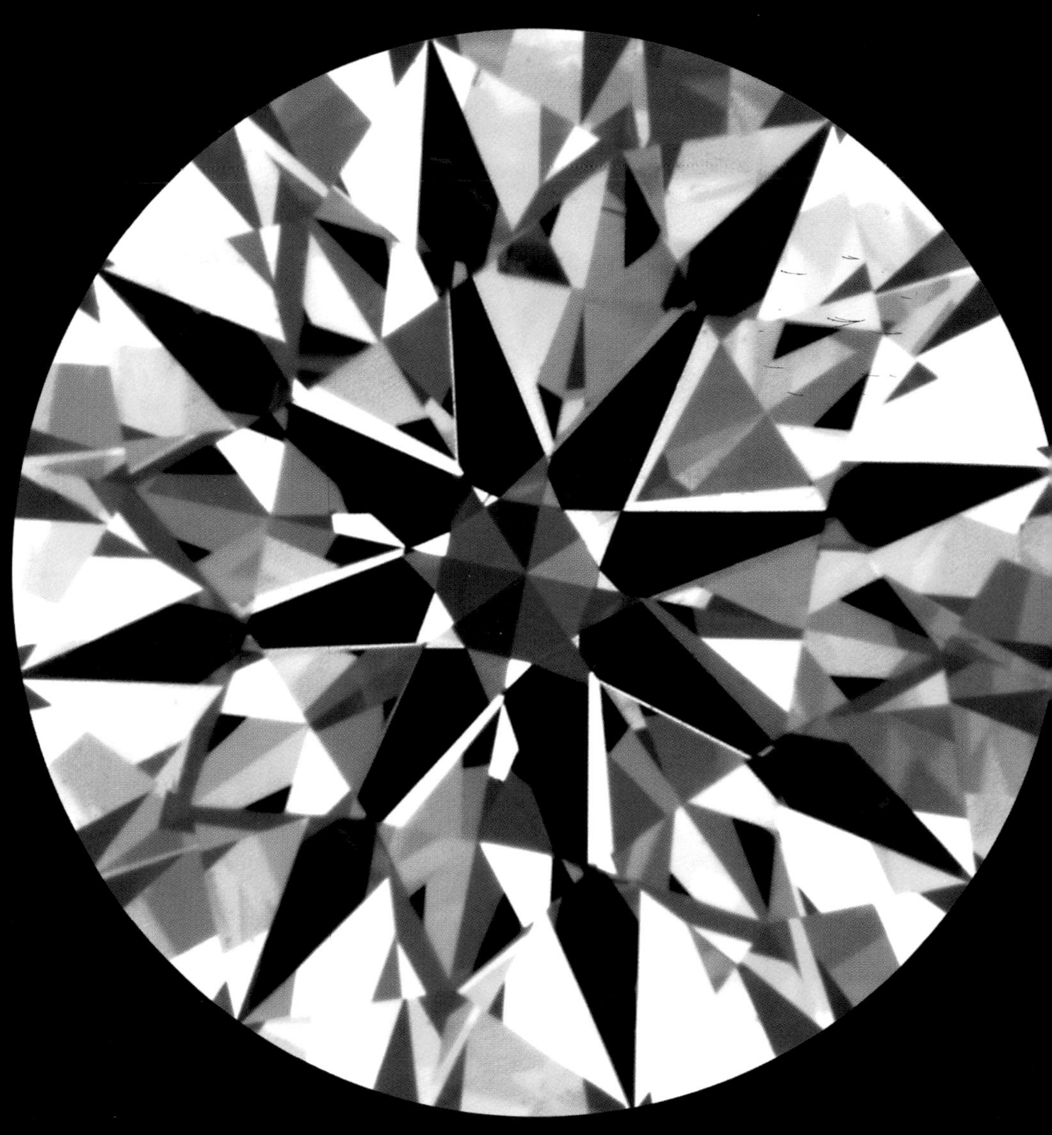

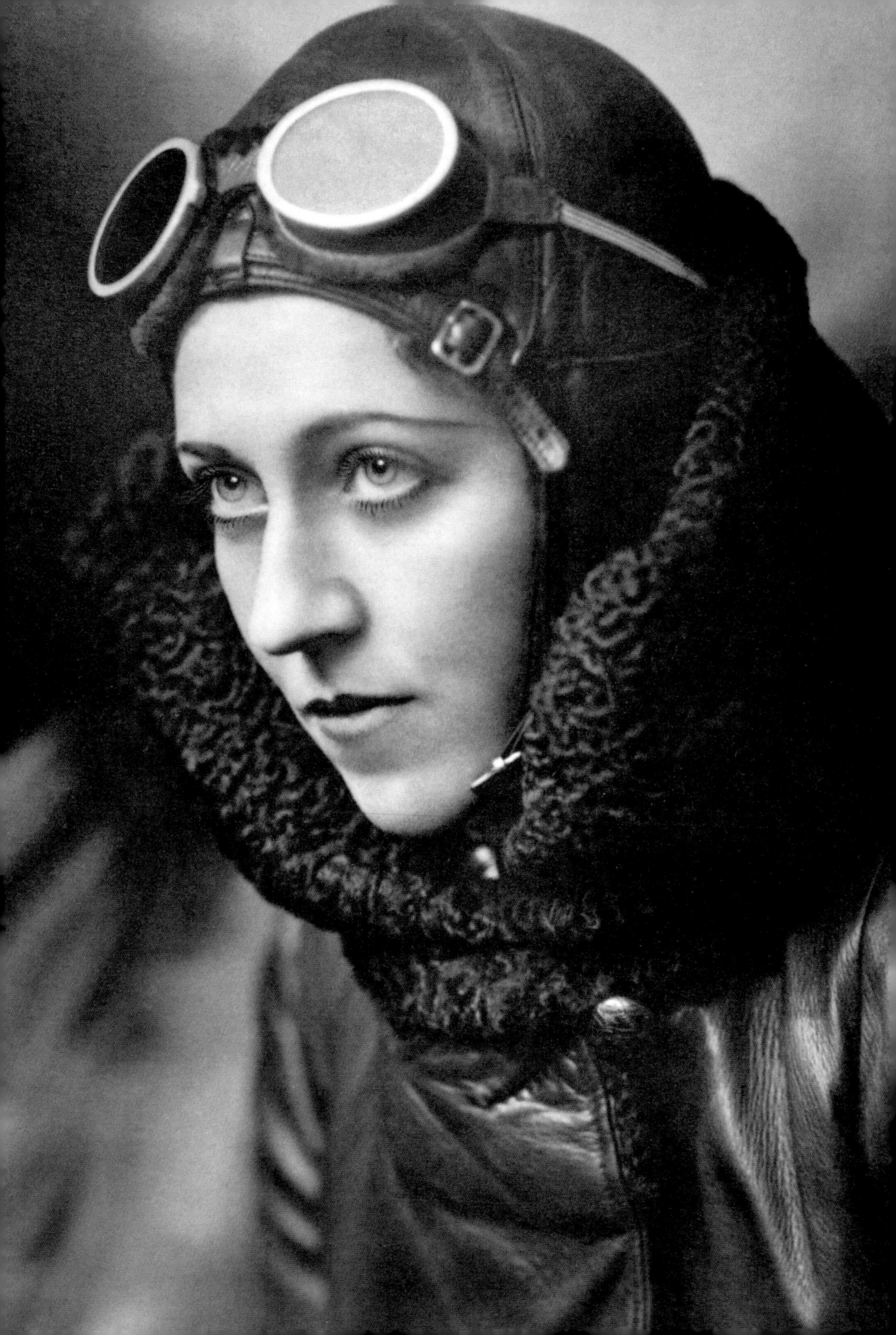

N 846	N 846	1 Monogramme *G S* Platine et roses. Couronne de Comte. 5 perles Platine et roses pour porte feuille cuir.	
	Lacloche	Commandé le 17 Janvier 1914.	
	LIVRÉ	Livré le	
N 847	N 847	1 Monogramme *A M* Platine et roses. Bloc lettres sur Jumelle écaille.	
AM	*Lacloche*	Commandé le 20 Janvier 1914	
	LIVRÉ	Livré le	
N 848	N 848	1 Boîte ivoire gravé formant bouton électrique.	
	Cartier		
	LIVRÉ	Commandé le 20 Janvier 1914. Livré le 31 Janvier 1914.	99
N 849 bis **849** bis	N 849 .849 bis	1 Nécessaire onyx noir monture or et platine.	
	Cartier		
	LIVRÉ	Commandé le 20 Janvier 1914. Livré le 28 Mars 1914	2362
N 850	N 850	1 Pendant platine joaillerie brillants et roses –	
	Templier Hallingre		
	LIVRÉ	Commandé le 22 Janvier 1914. Livré le 20 Février 1914.	

N°	Maison	Description	Prix
N°851	Templier Hallingre — LIVRÉ	1 Pendant platine joaillerie brillants et roses. Commandé le 22 Janvier 1914. Livré le 20 Février 1914	
N°852	Stock — LIVRÉ — Boucheron	Pendentif Saphir joaillerie brill^{ts}, juni en lune. Commandé le 24 Janvier 1914. Livré le Juillet 1918.	5180
N°853	Bancelin — LIVRÉ	1 Médaillon platine et onyx noir, centre cristal gravé — Commandé le 29 Janvier 1914. Livré le 5 Février 1914	85
N°854	Cartier — LIVRÉ	1 Boutons électrique ivoire gravé. Commandé le 29 Janvier 1914. Livré le 14 Février 1914	100
N°855	Tiffany C° — LIVRÉ	1 Nécessaire or et argent repoussé et guilloché — Commandé le 2 Février 1914. Livré le 9 Mars 1914	550

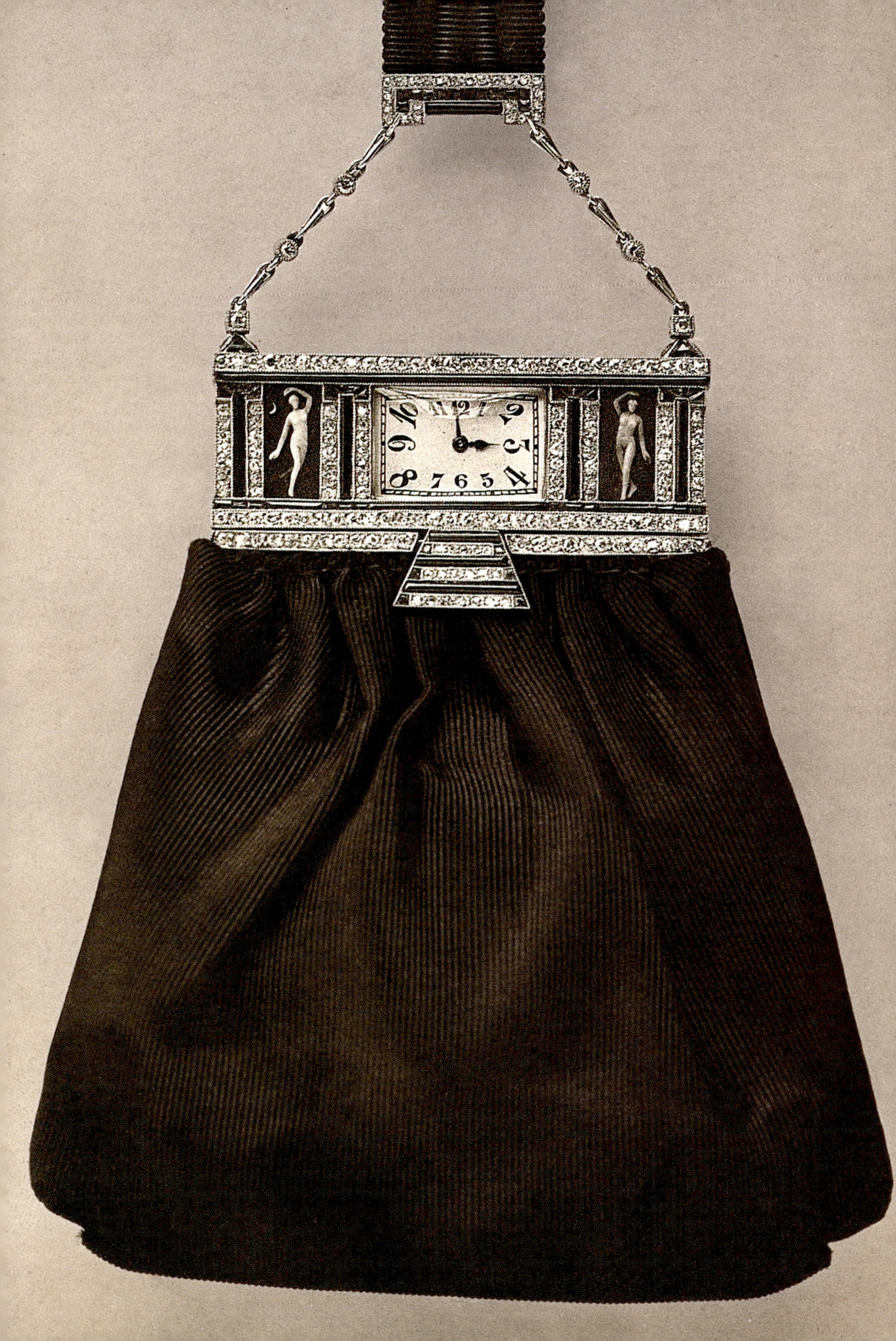

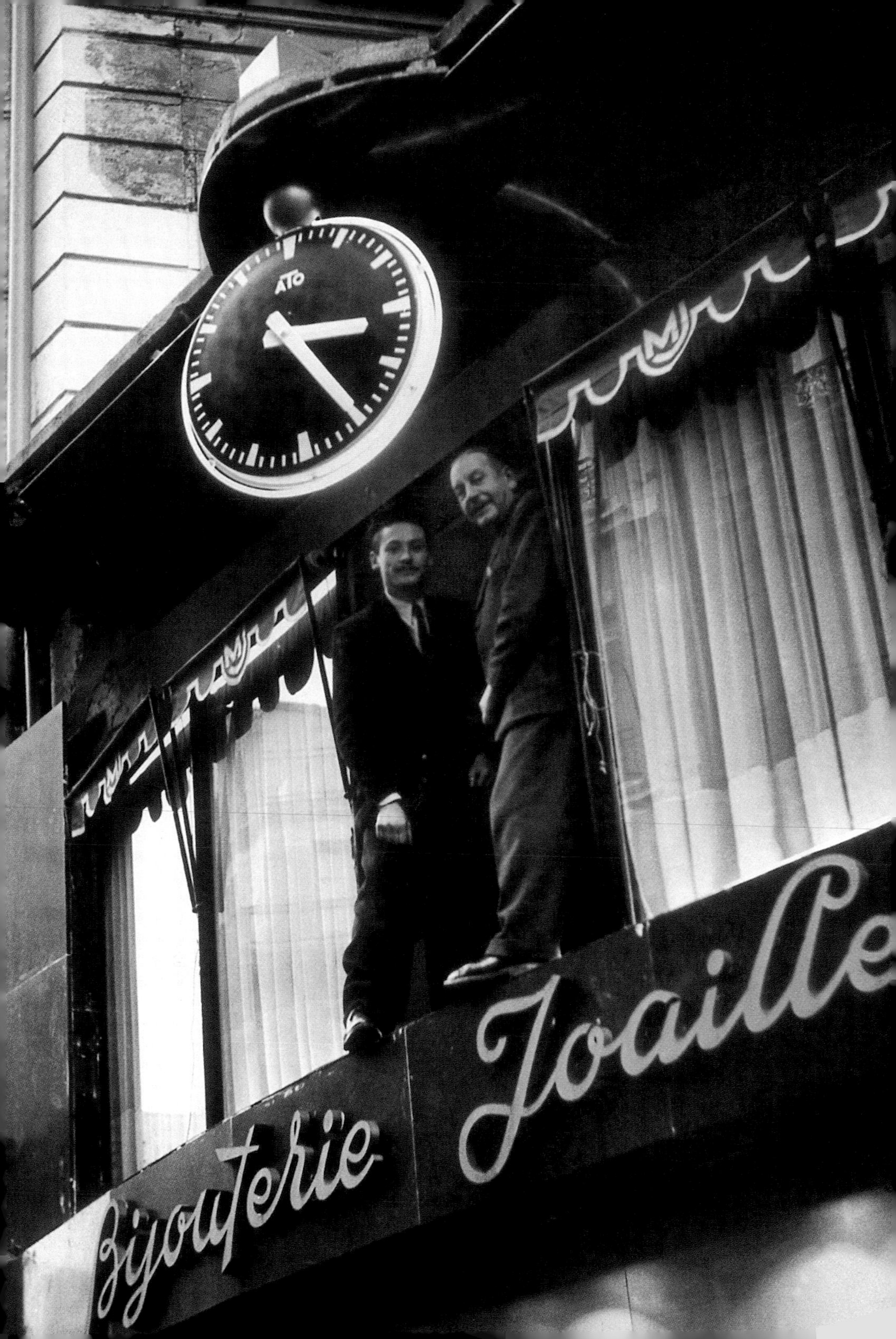

ATO
Bijouterie Joaille

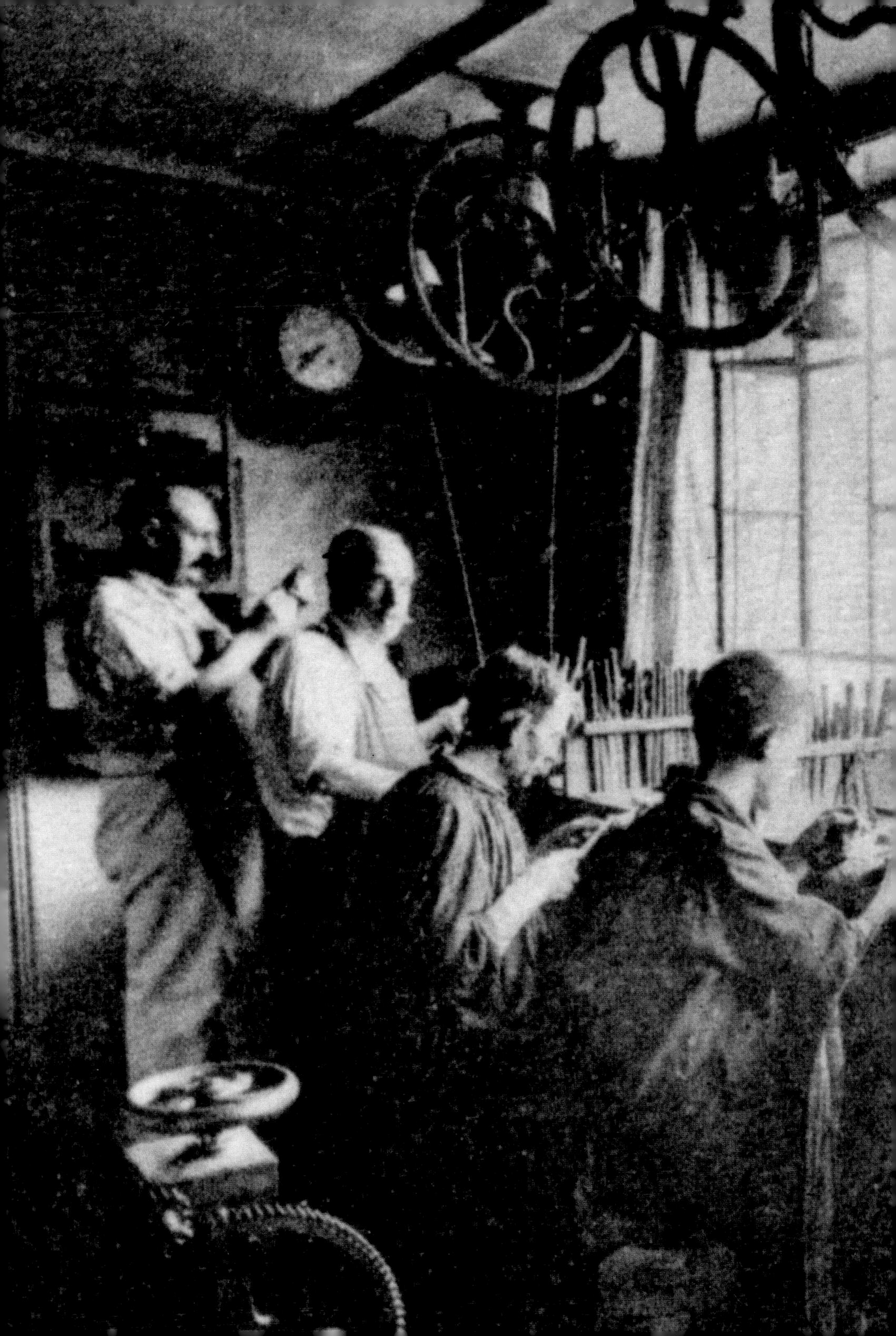

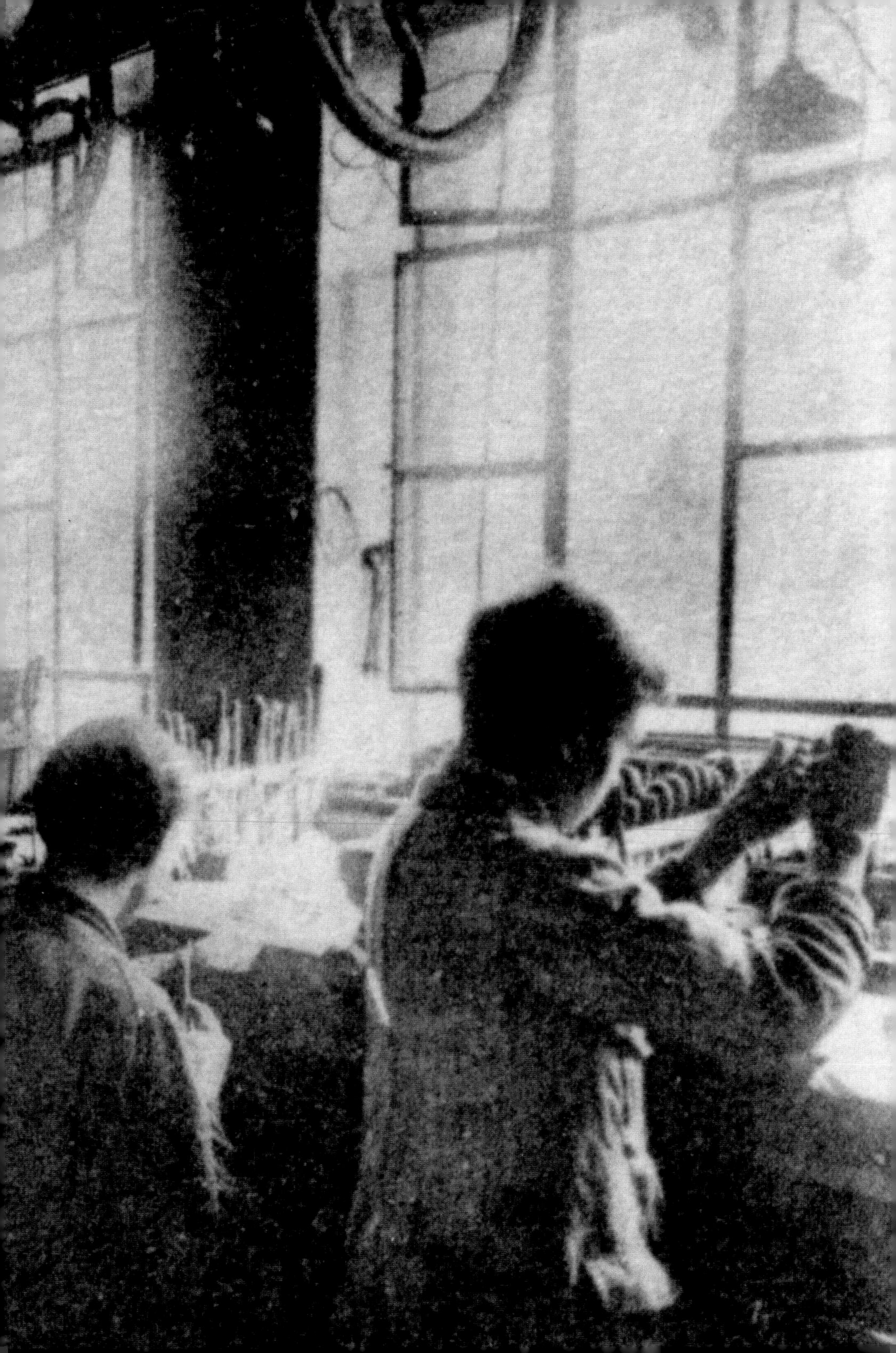

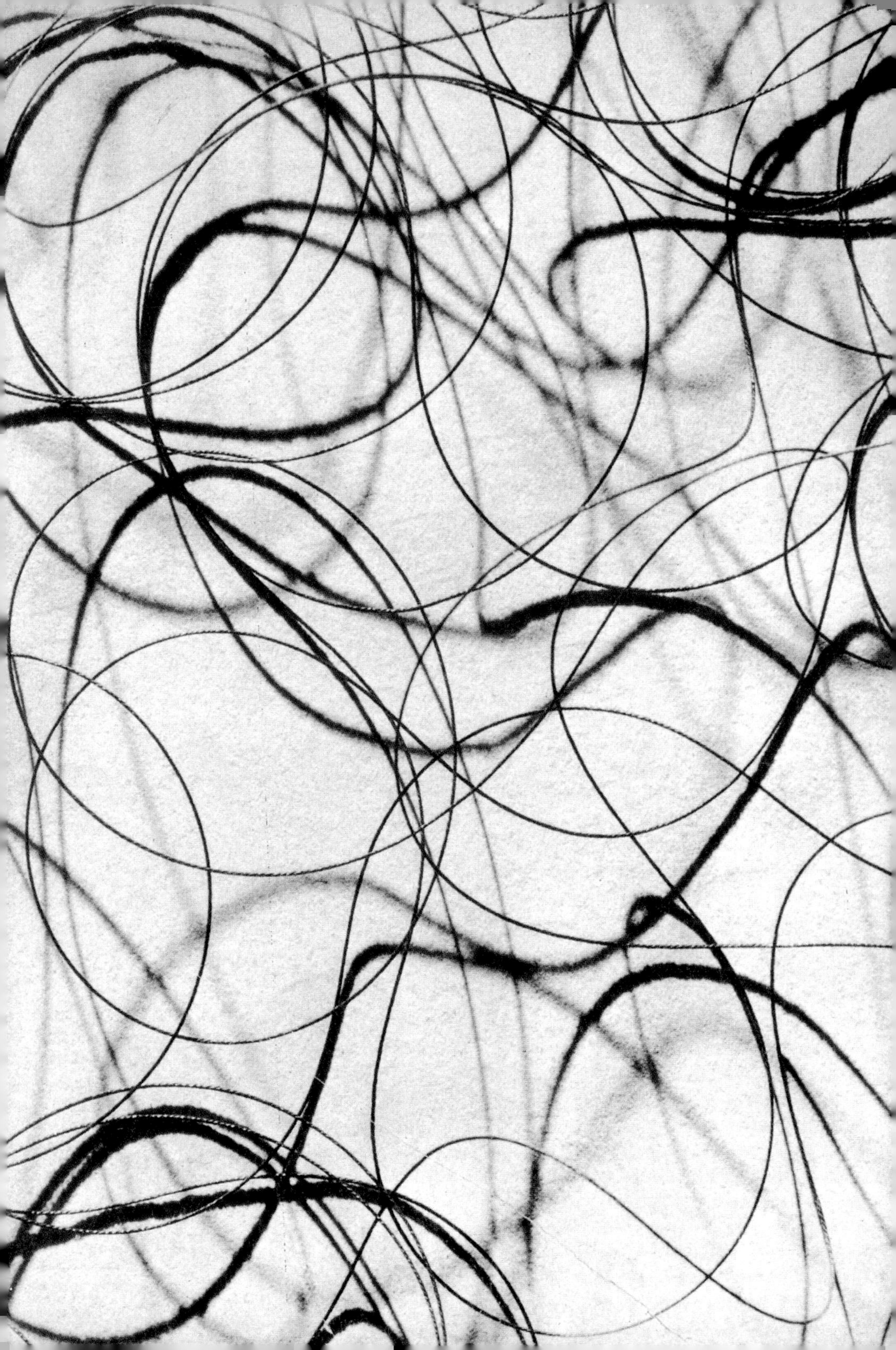

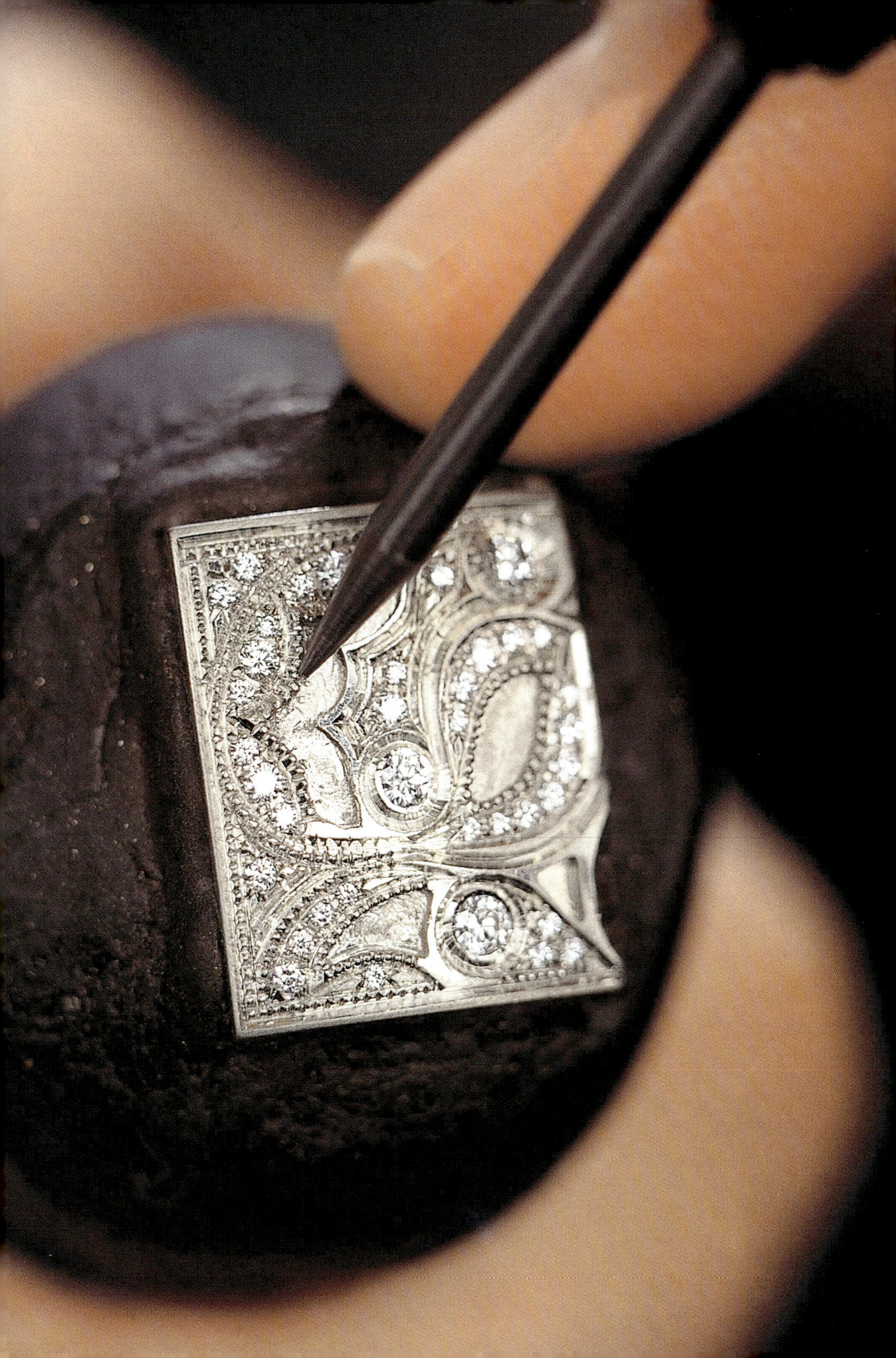

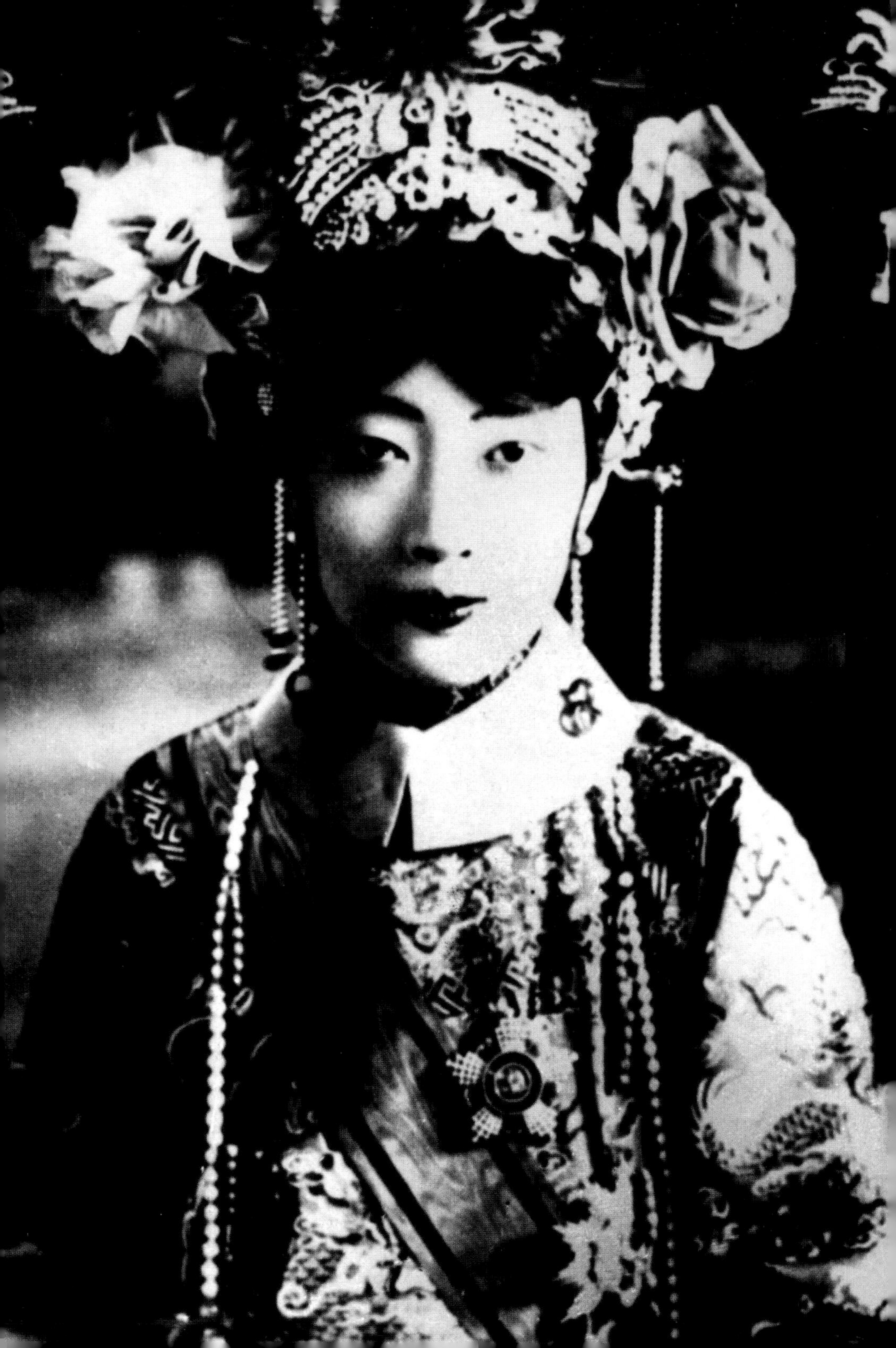

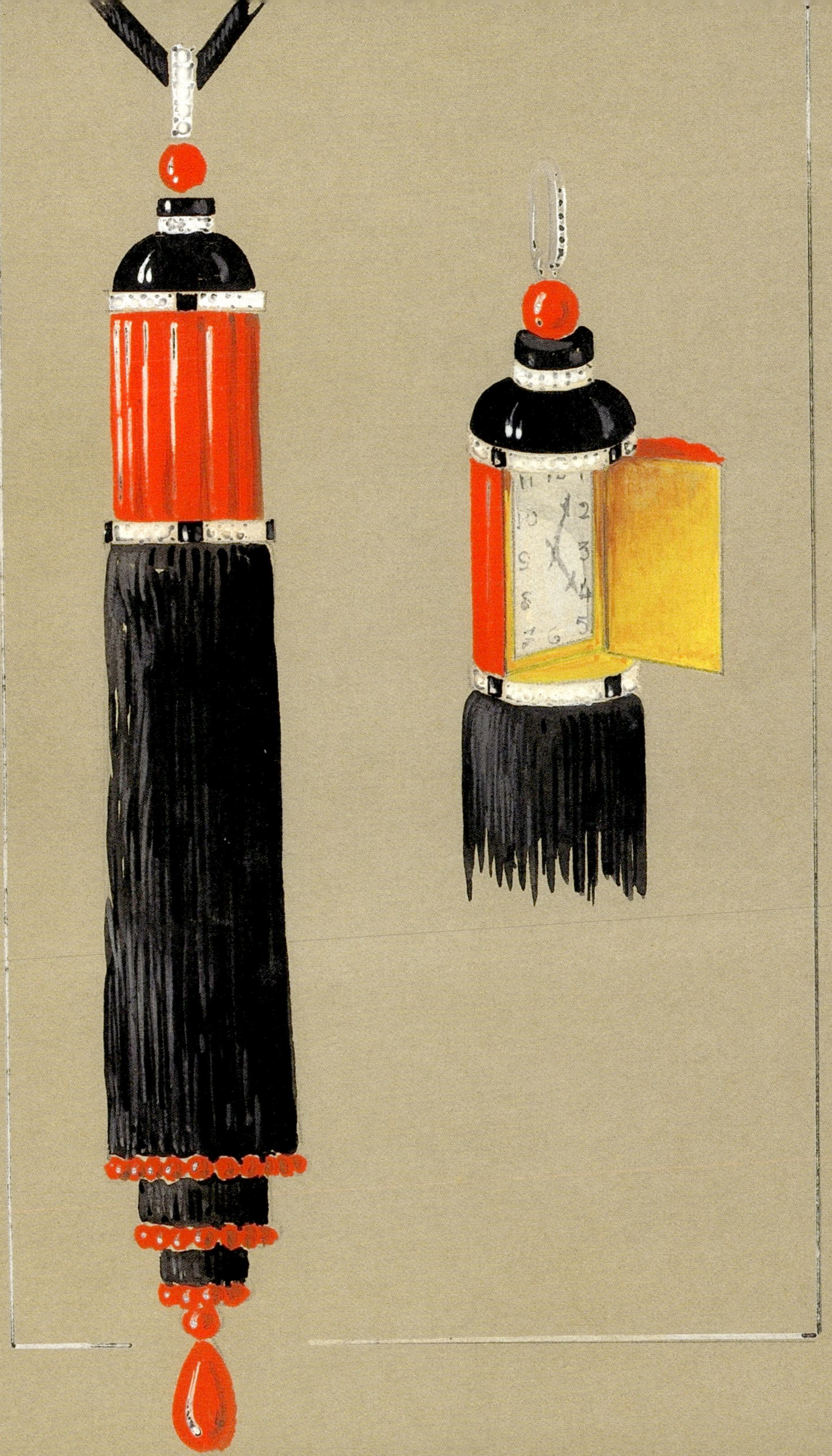

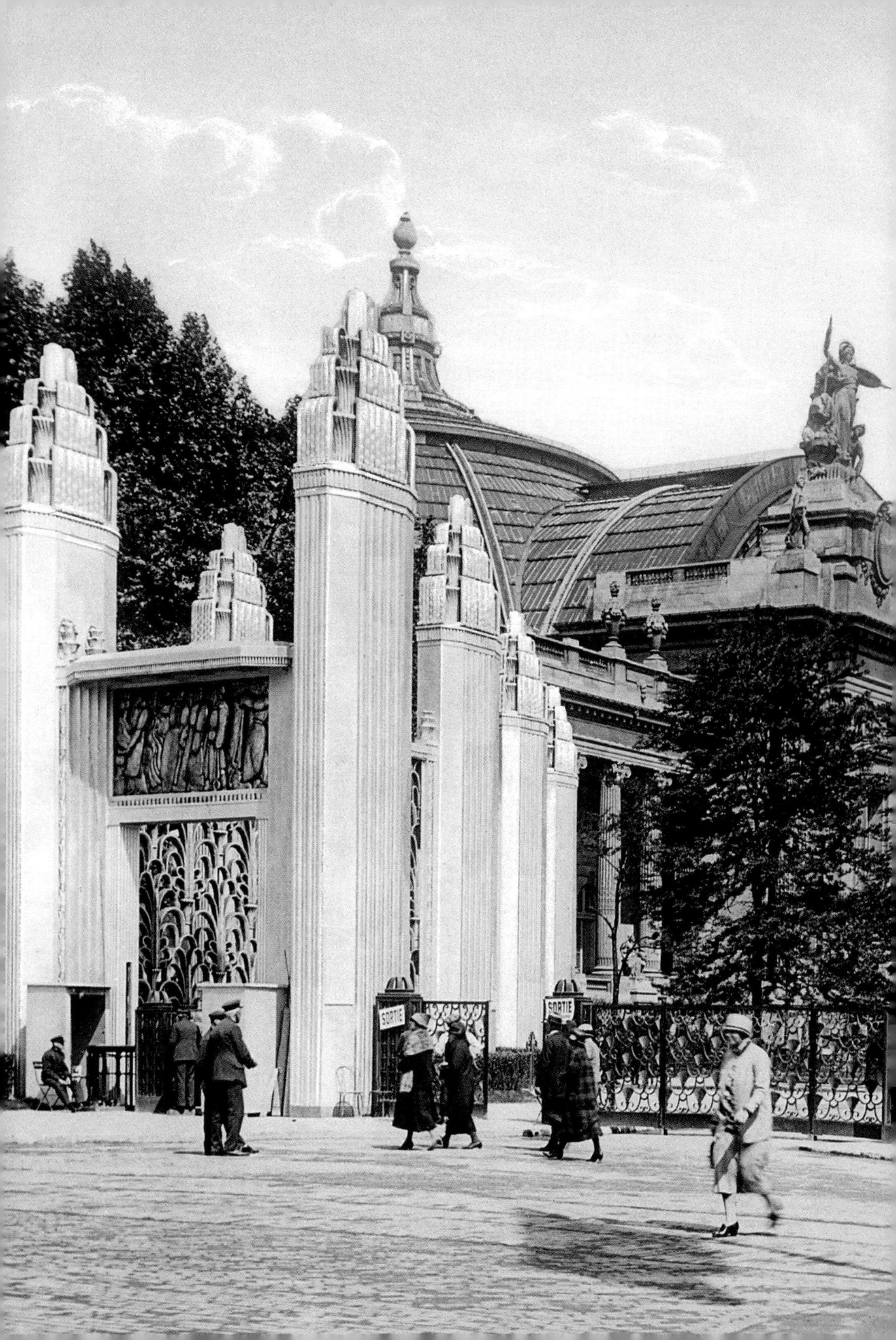

SORTIE
SORTIE

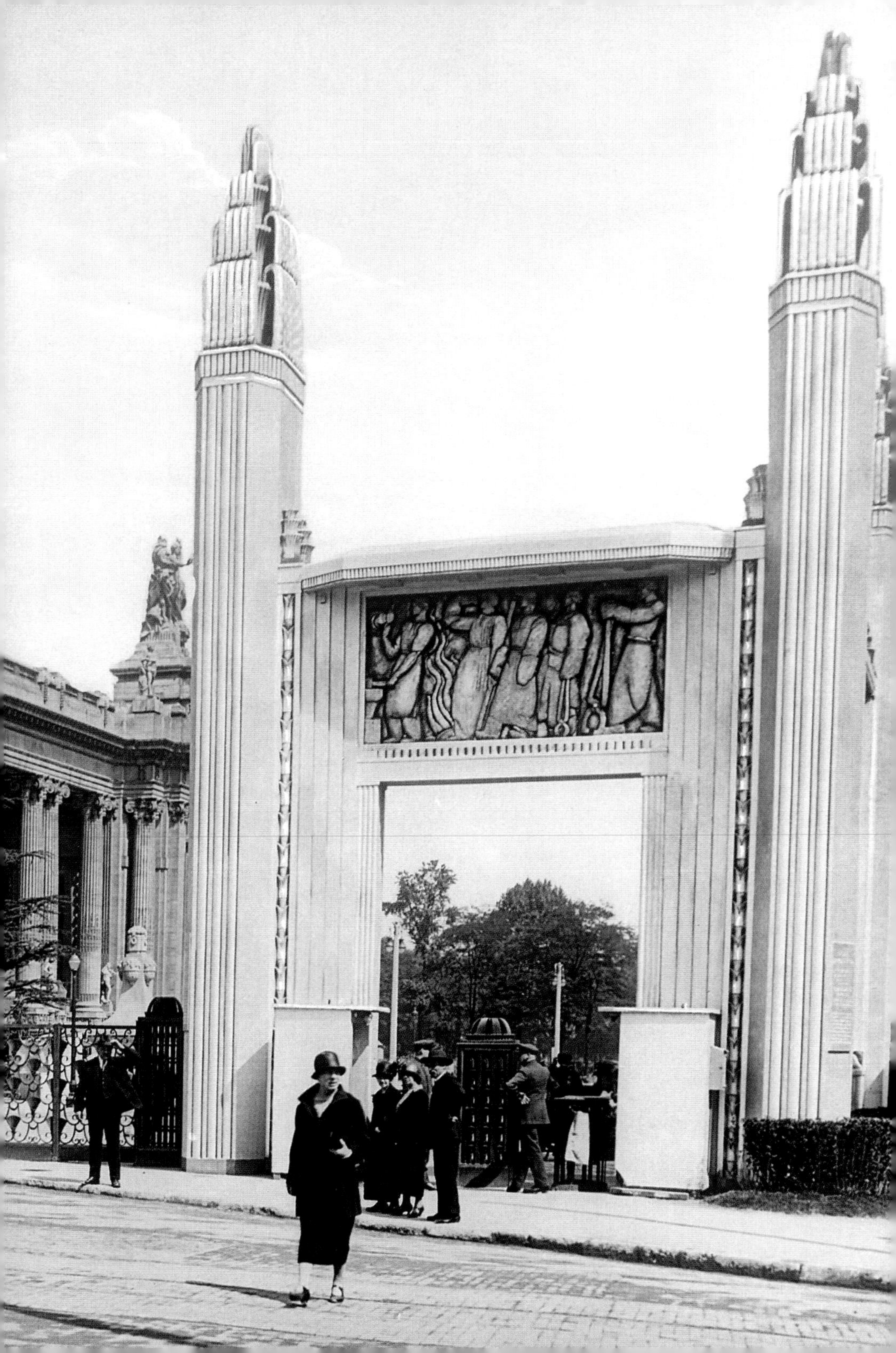

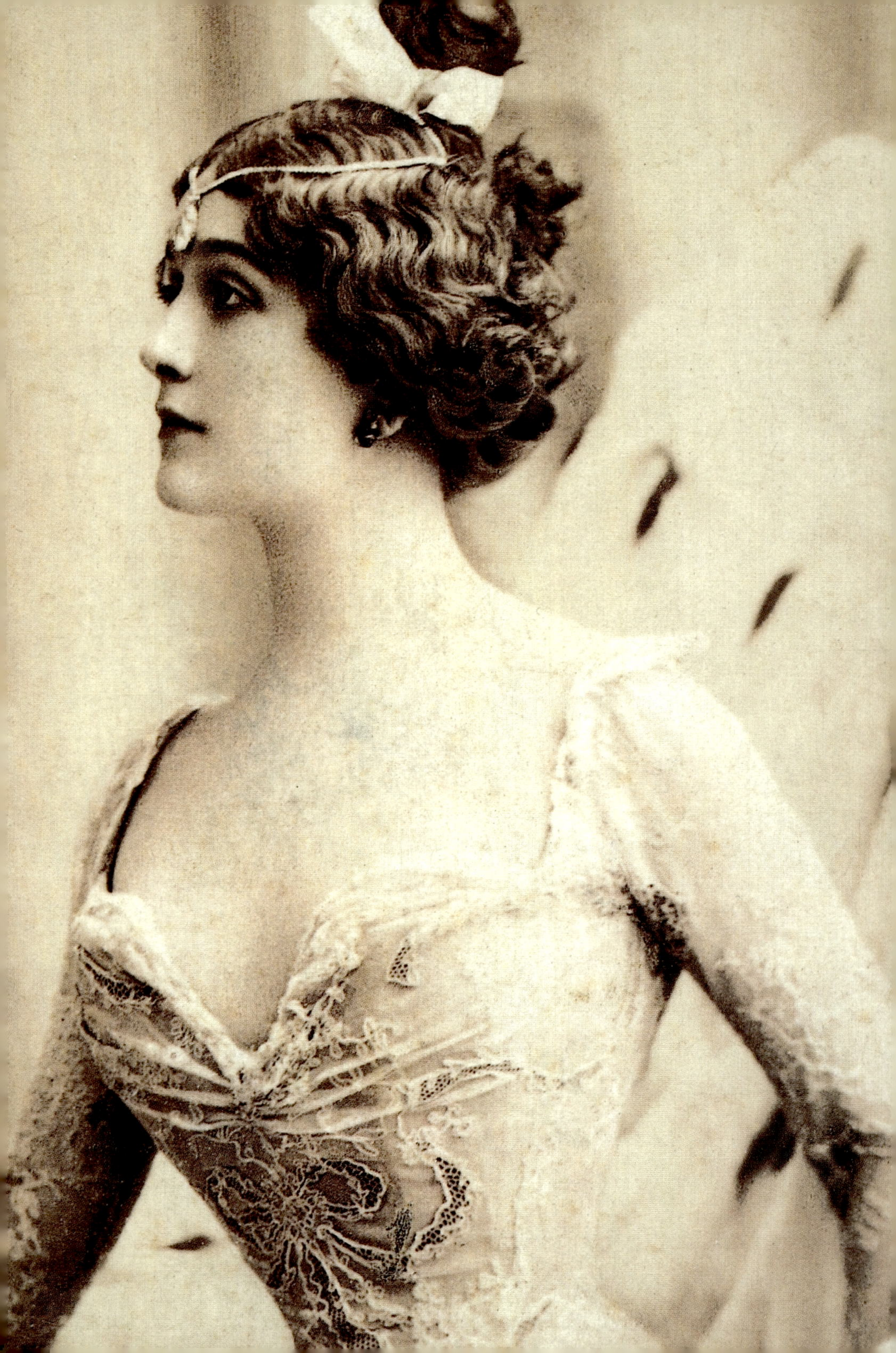

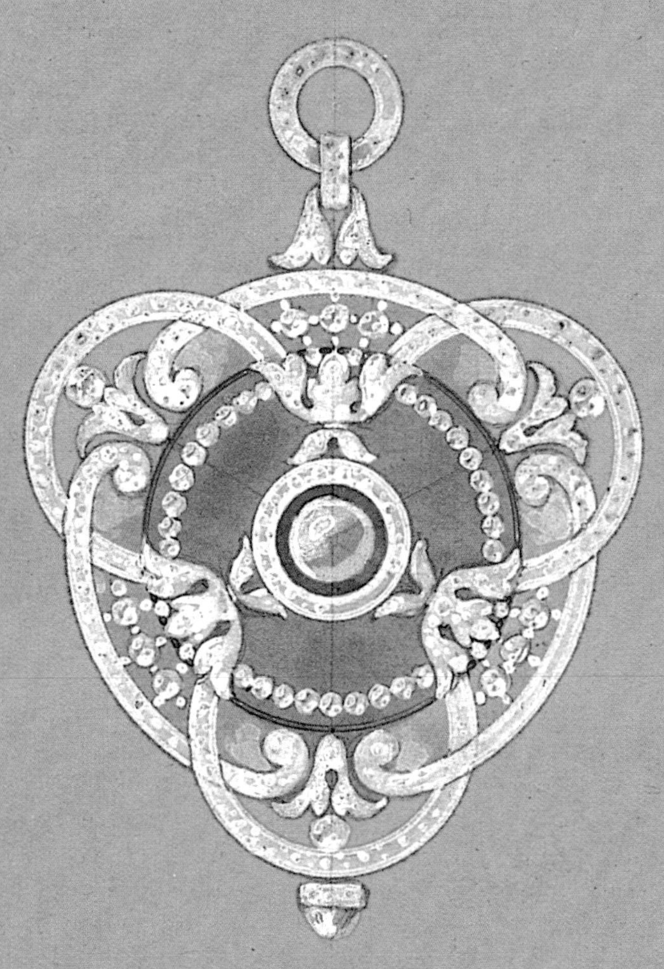

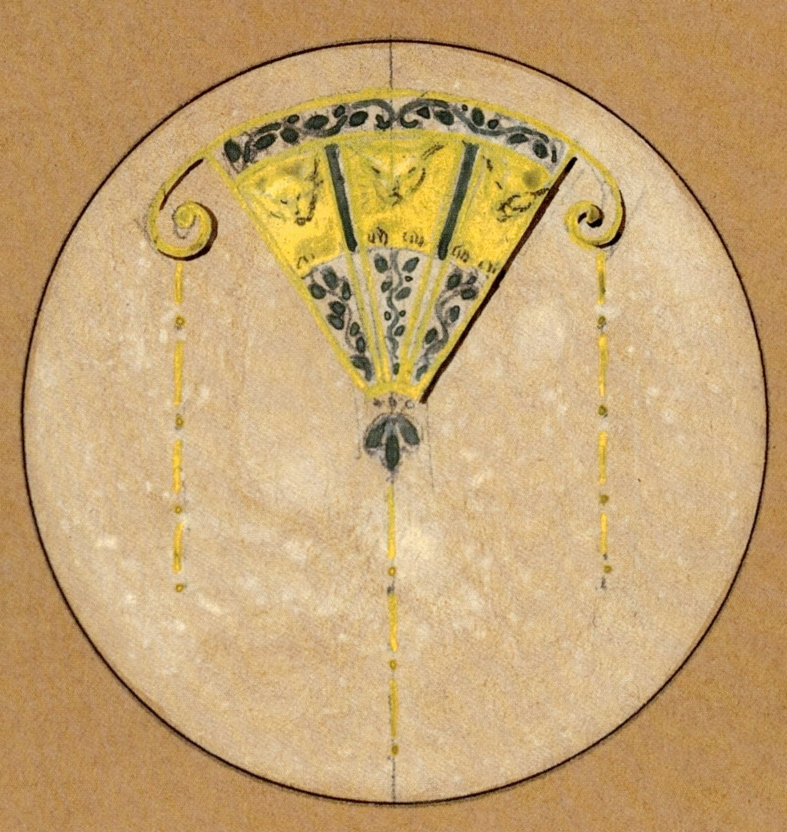

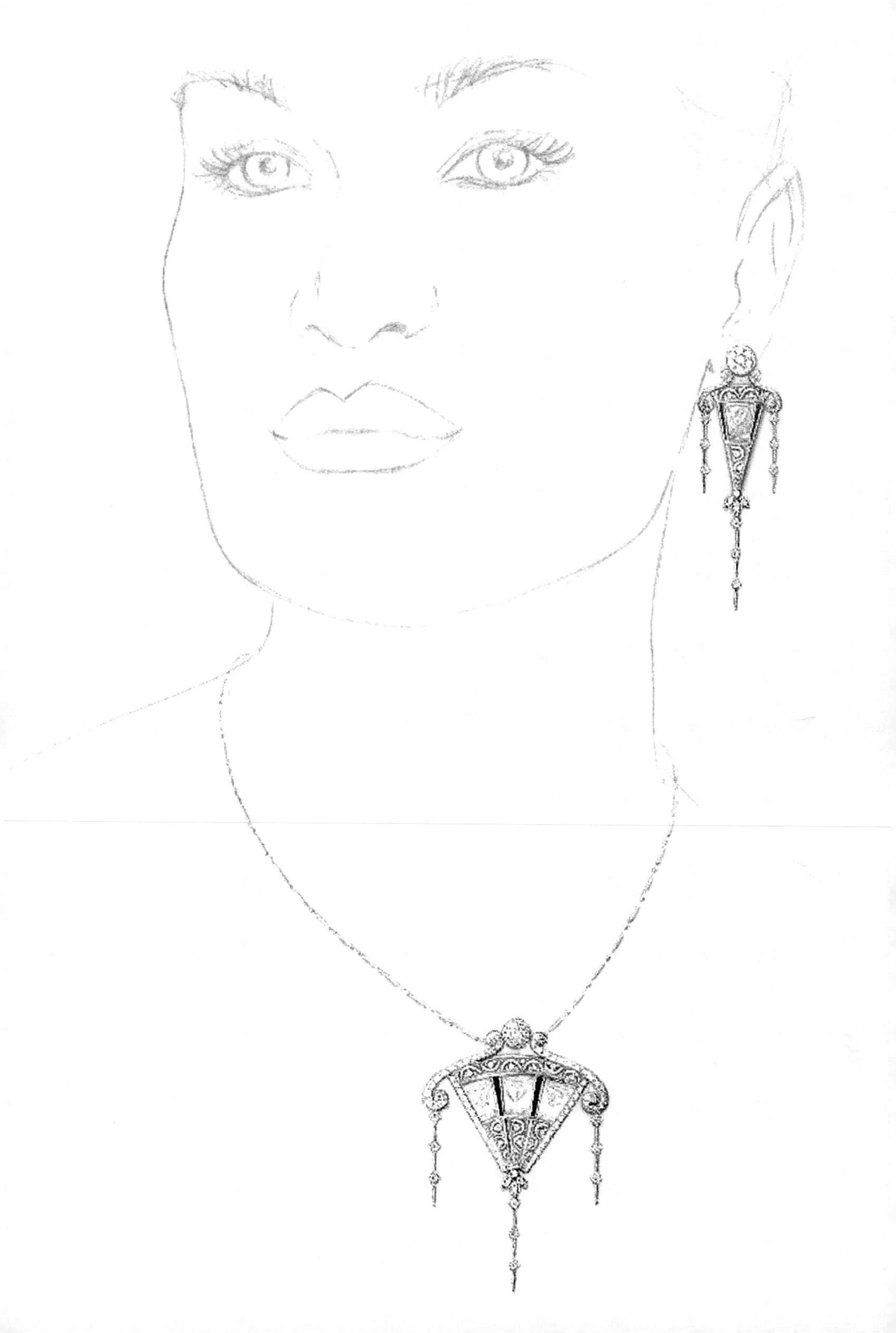

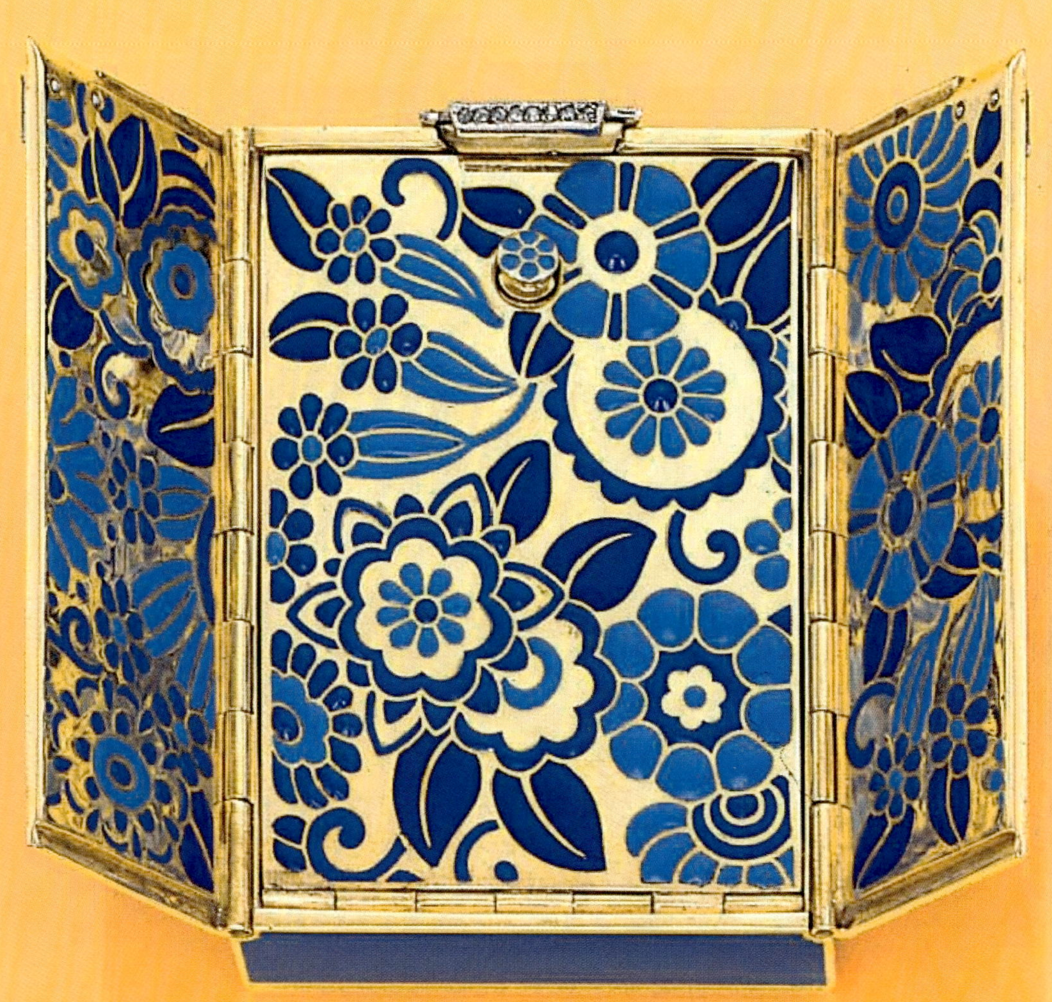

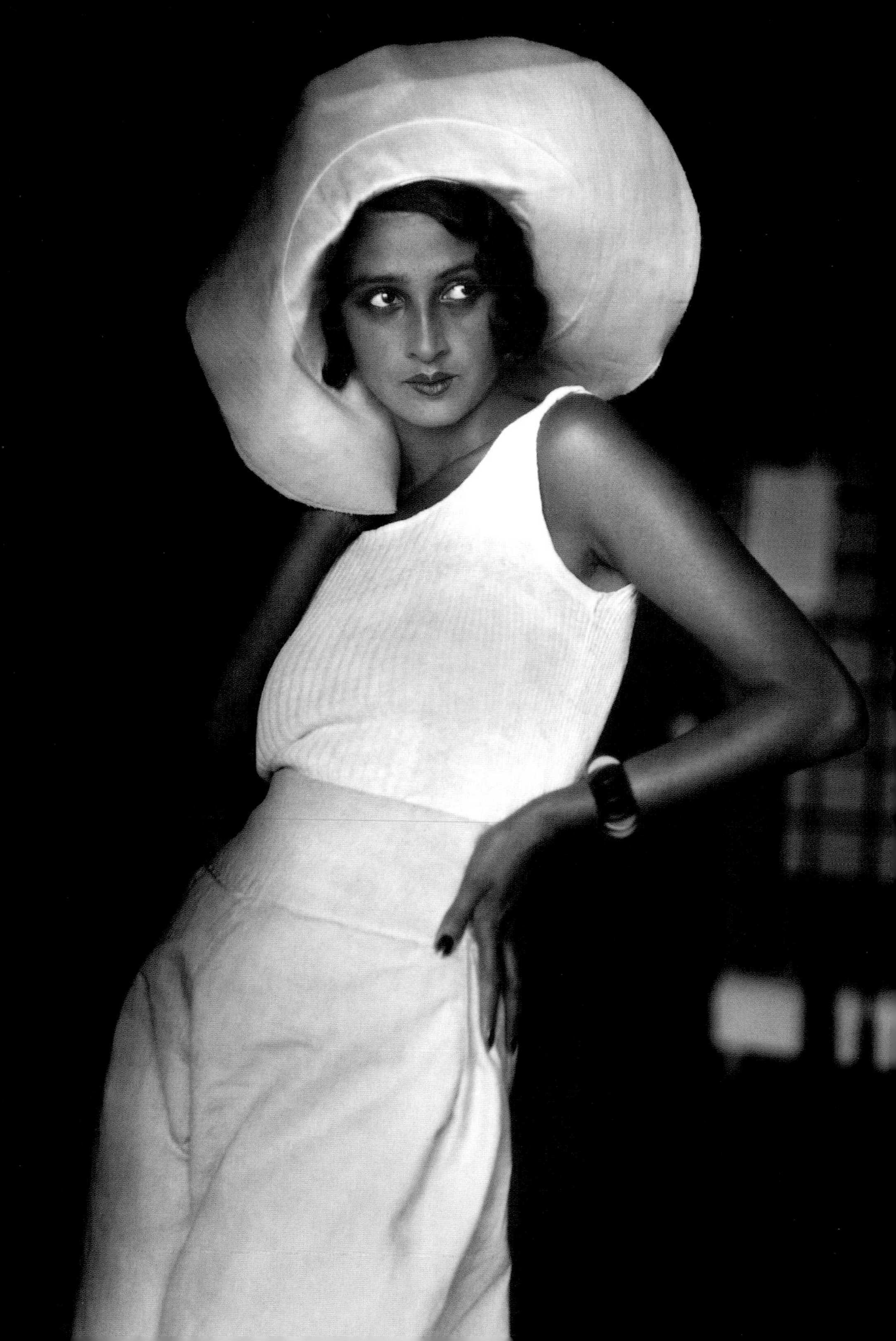

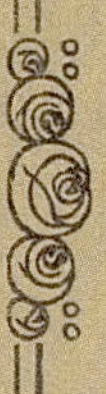

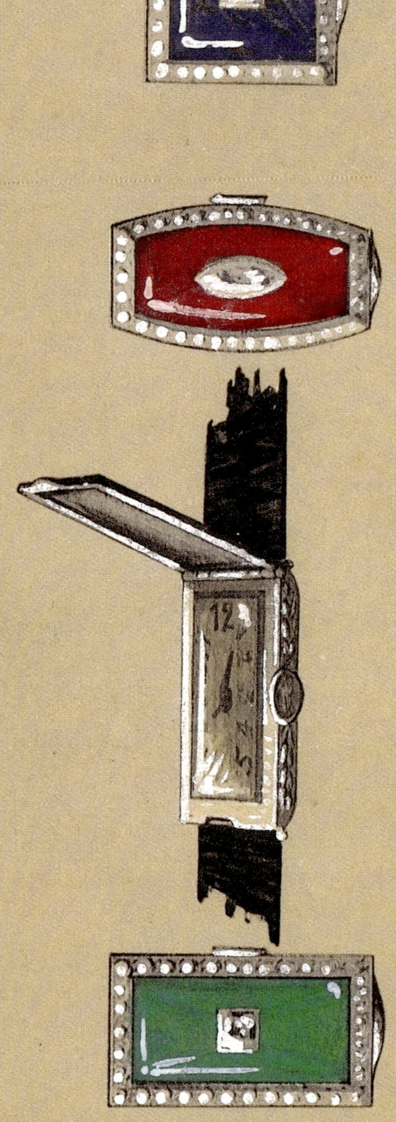

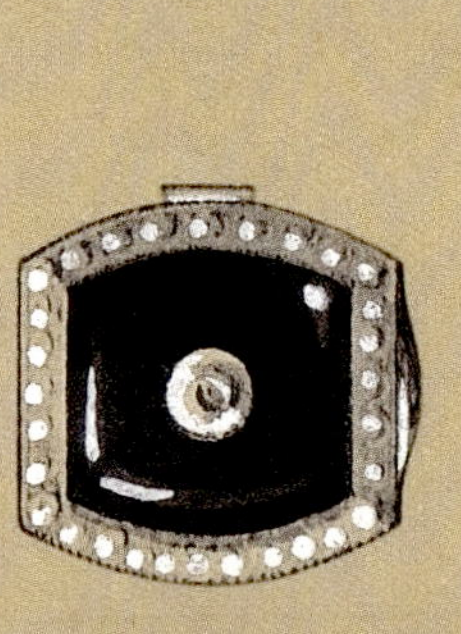

MONTRES BRACELETS OUVRANTES, BREVETÉ S. G. D. G.

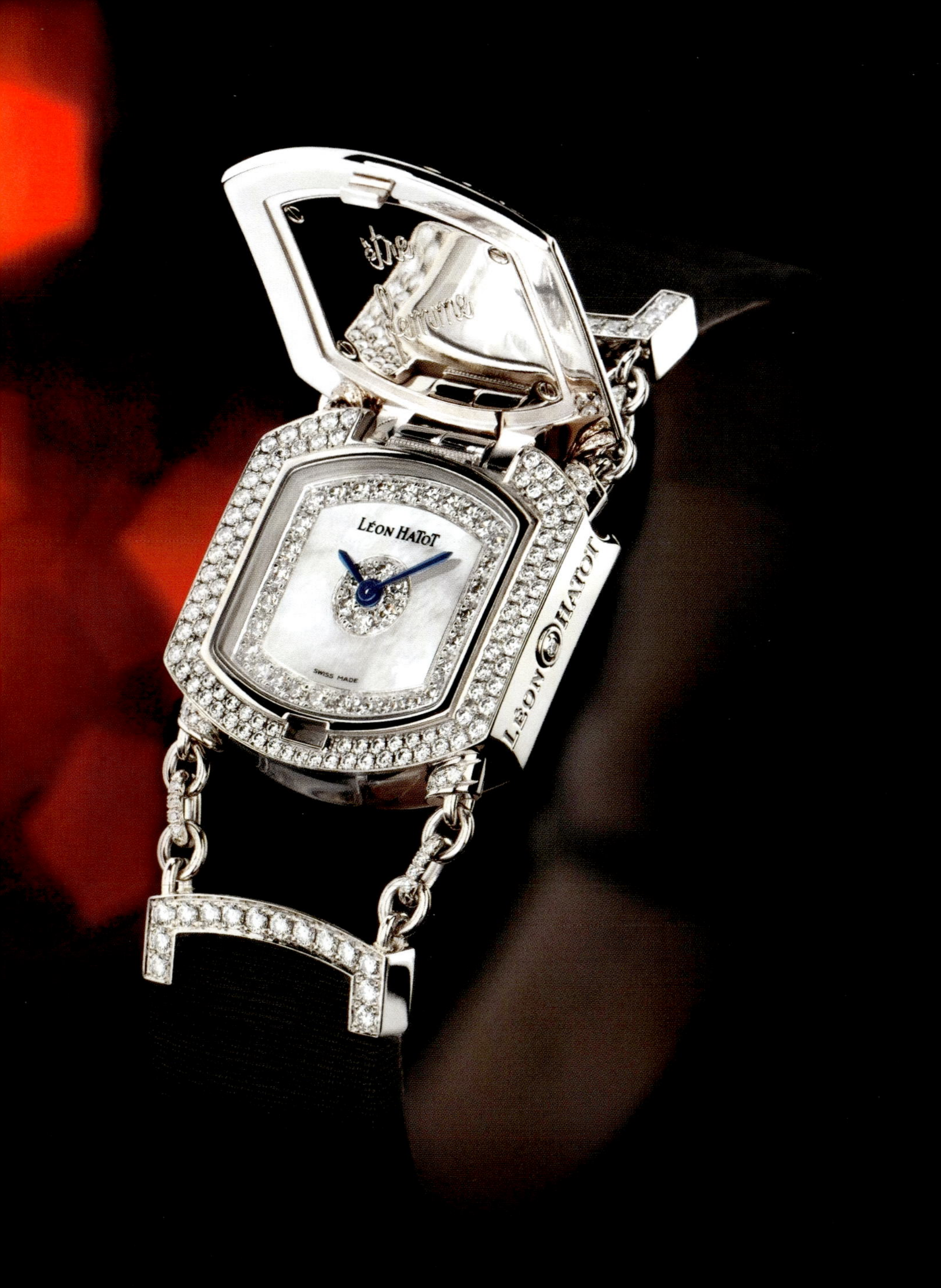

LÉON HATOT
SWISS MADE
LÉON HATOT

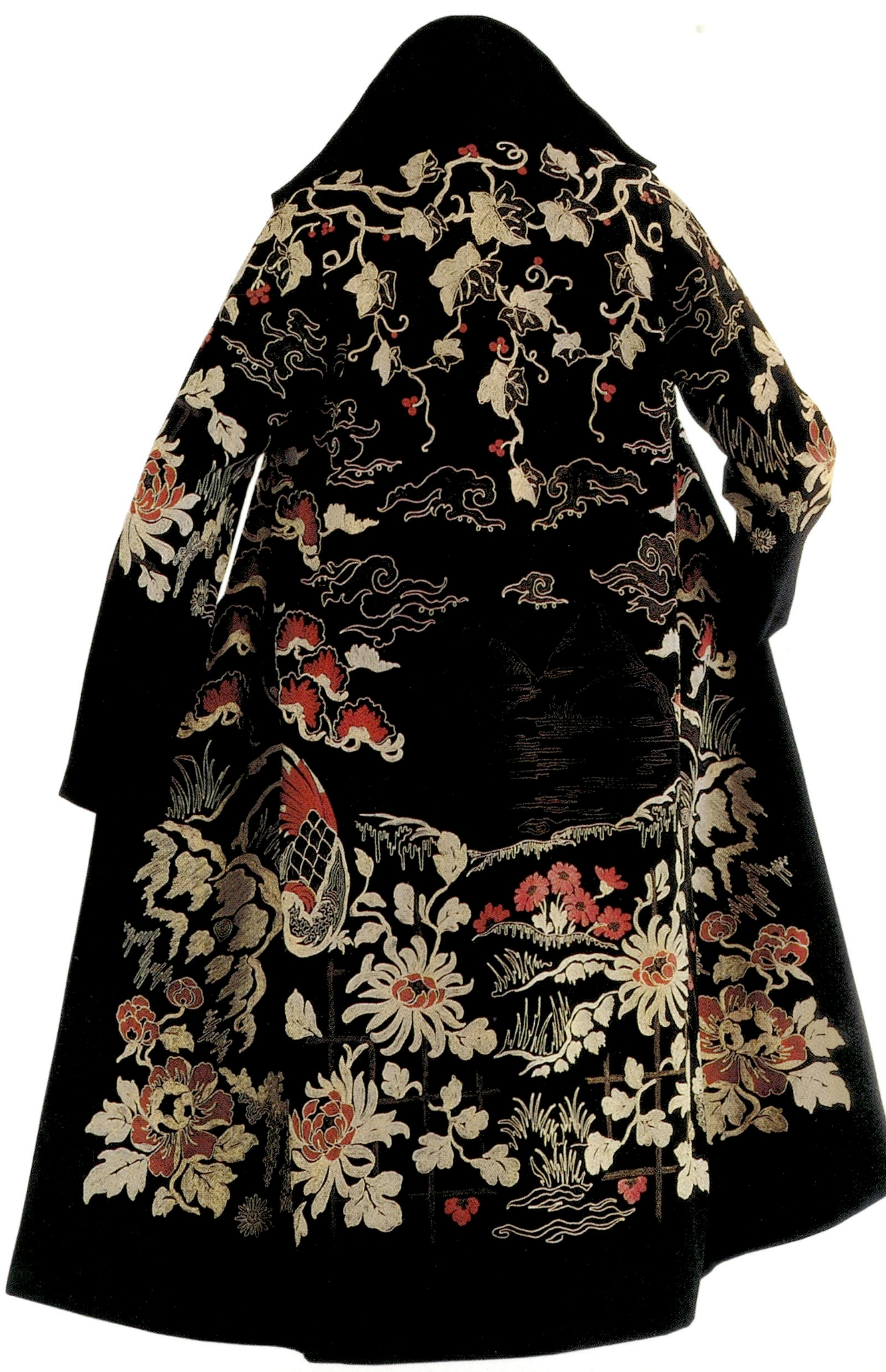

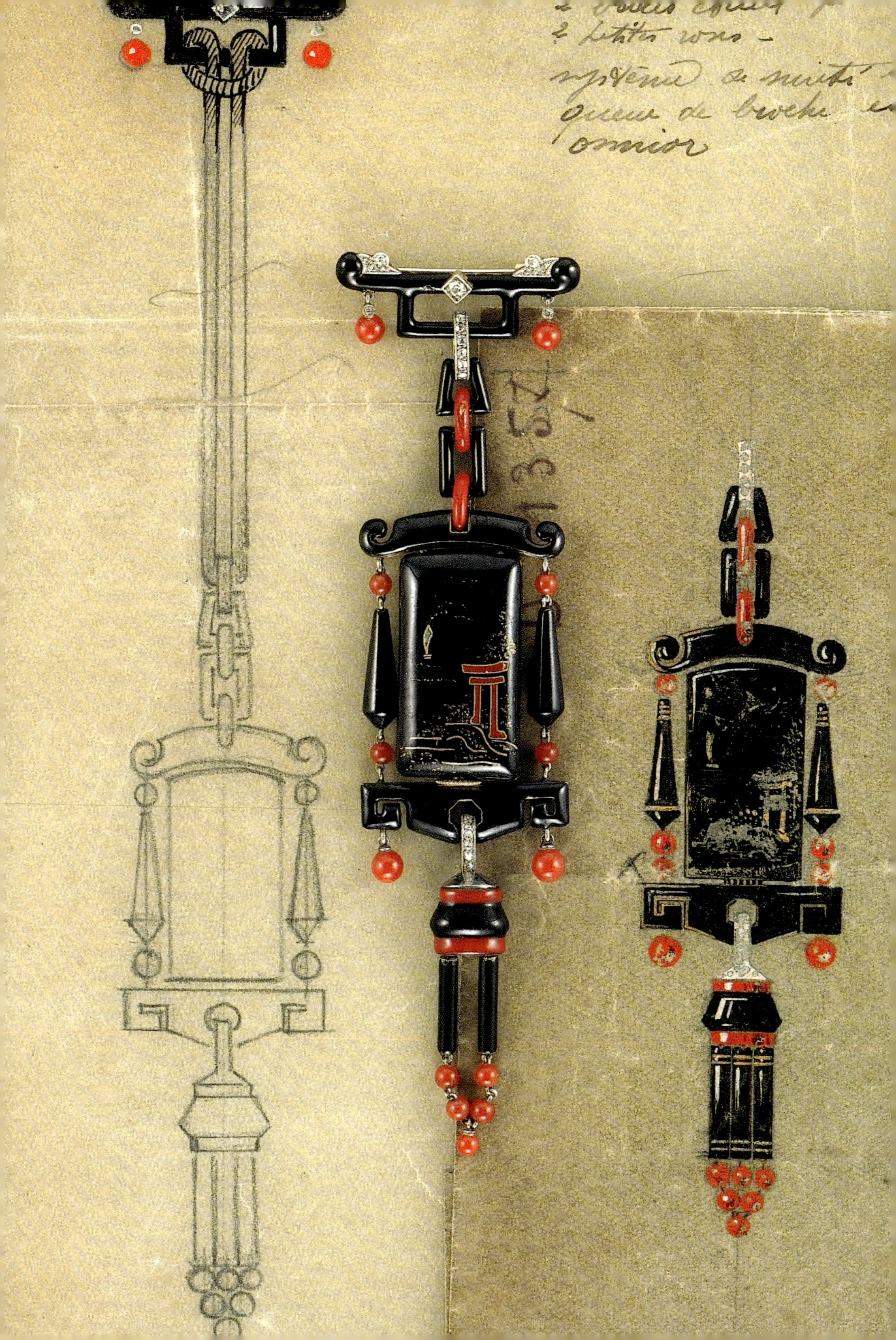

2 petites roues —
système de suite
queue de broche
ressort

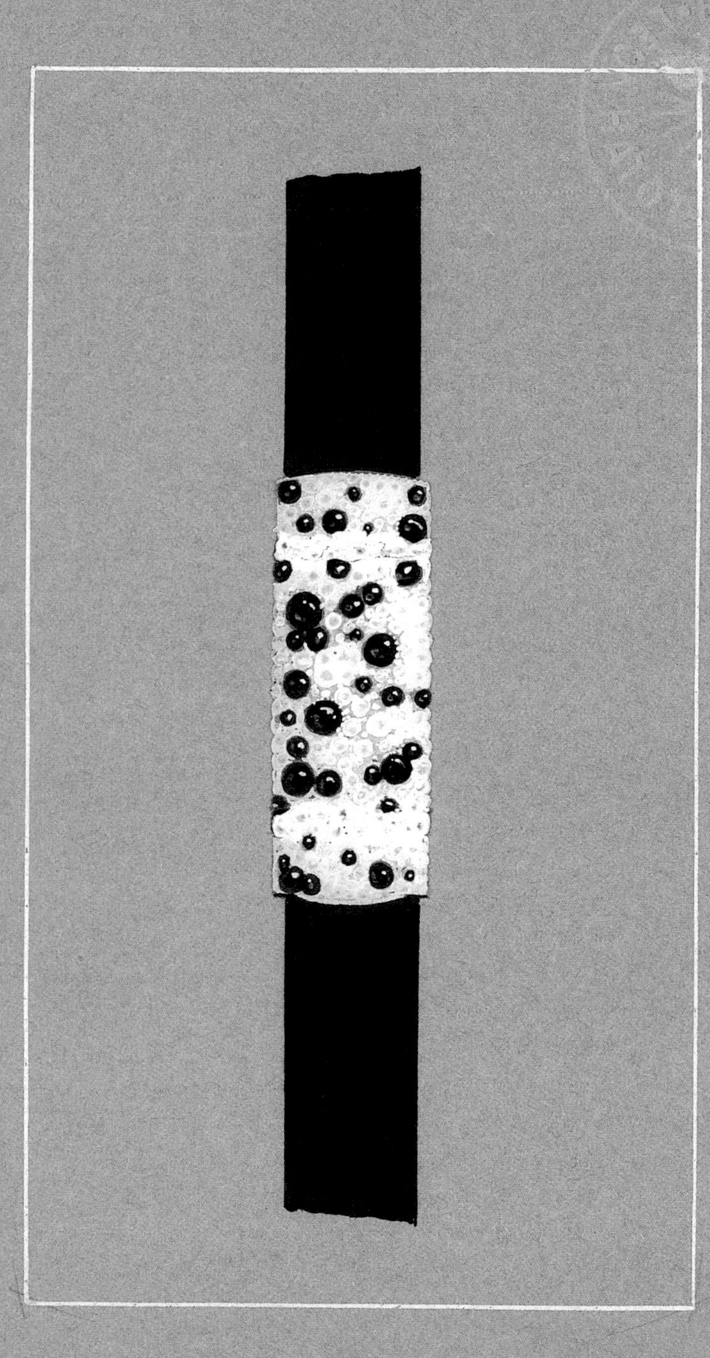

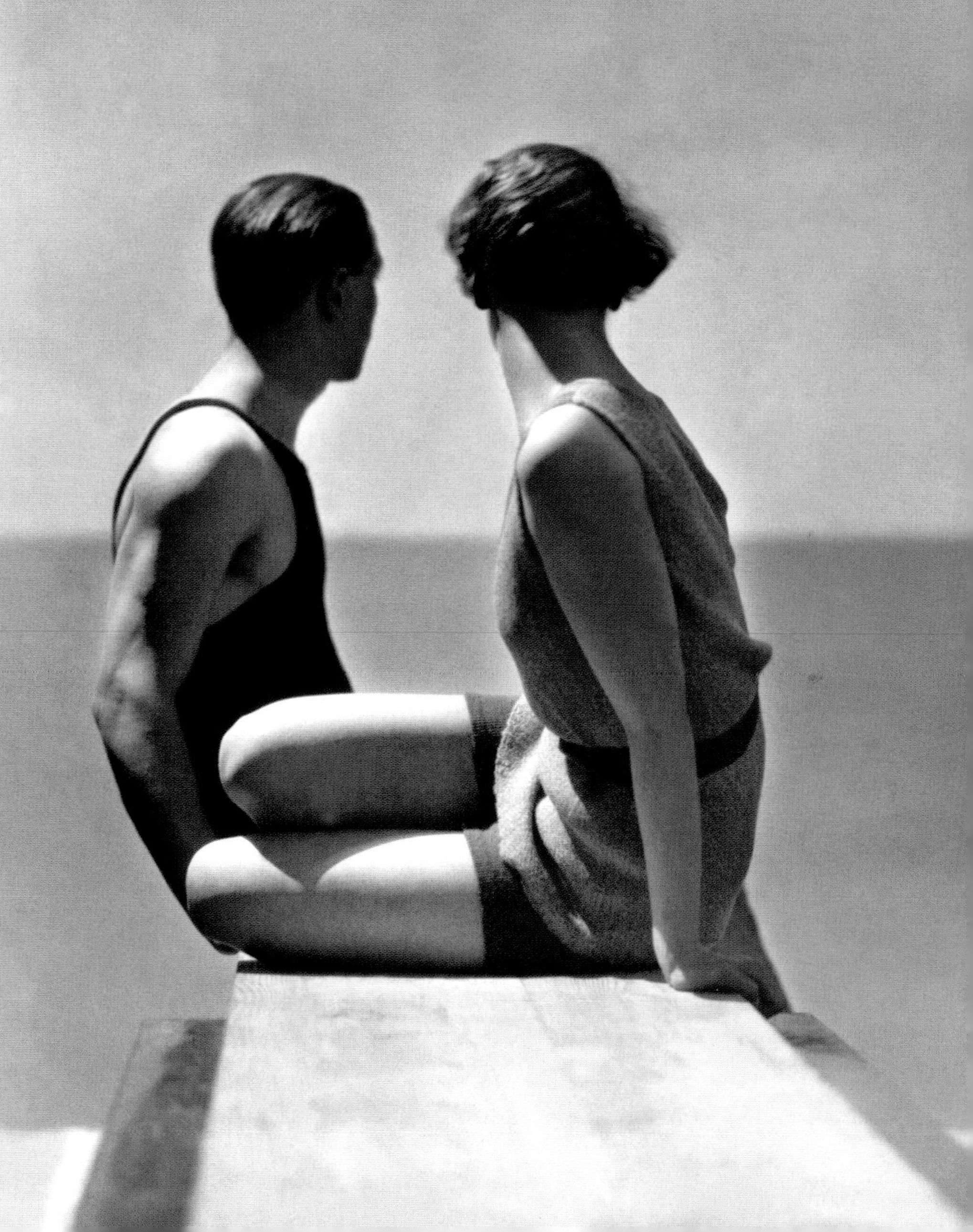

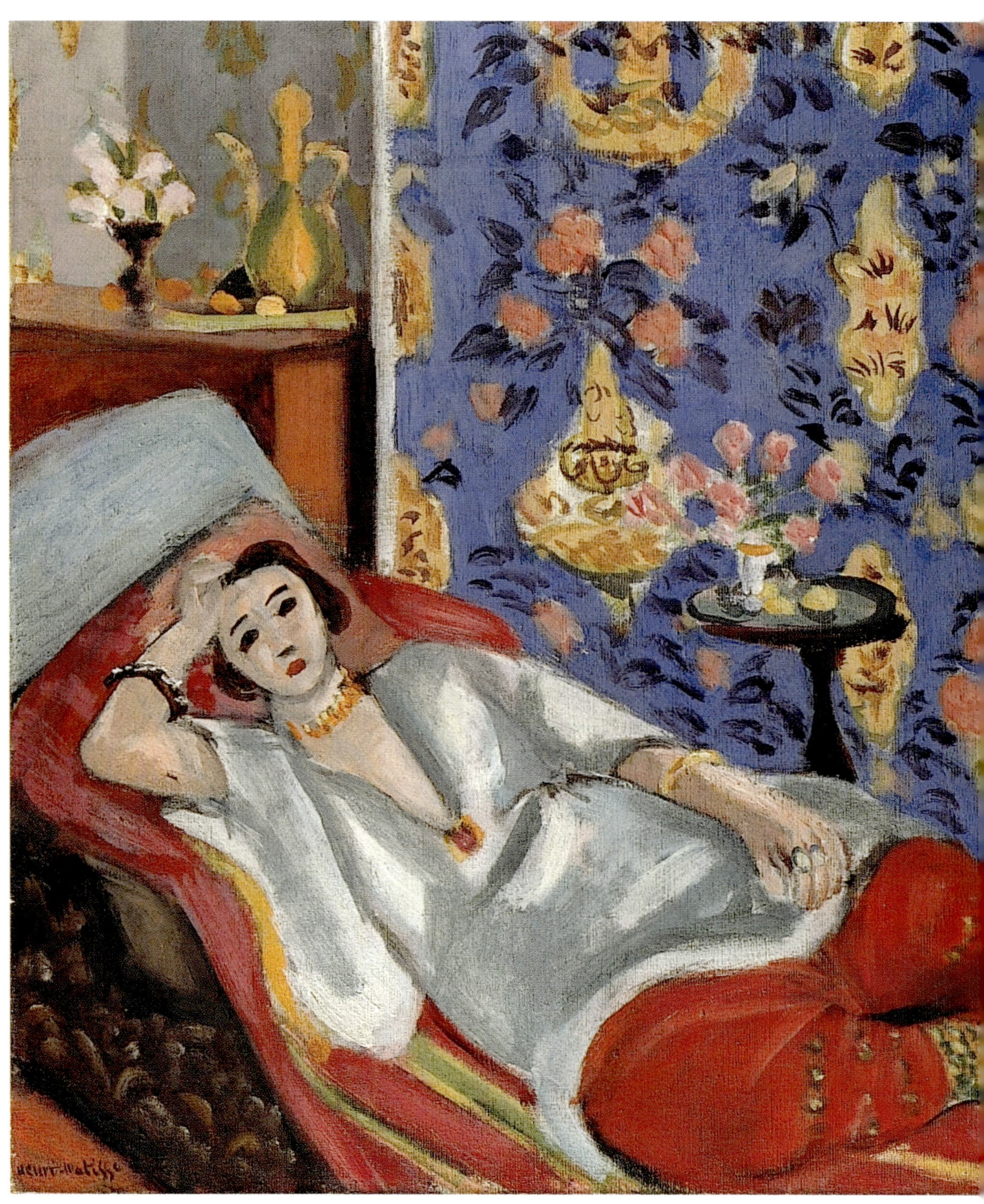
Henri-Matisse

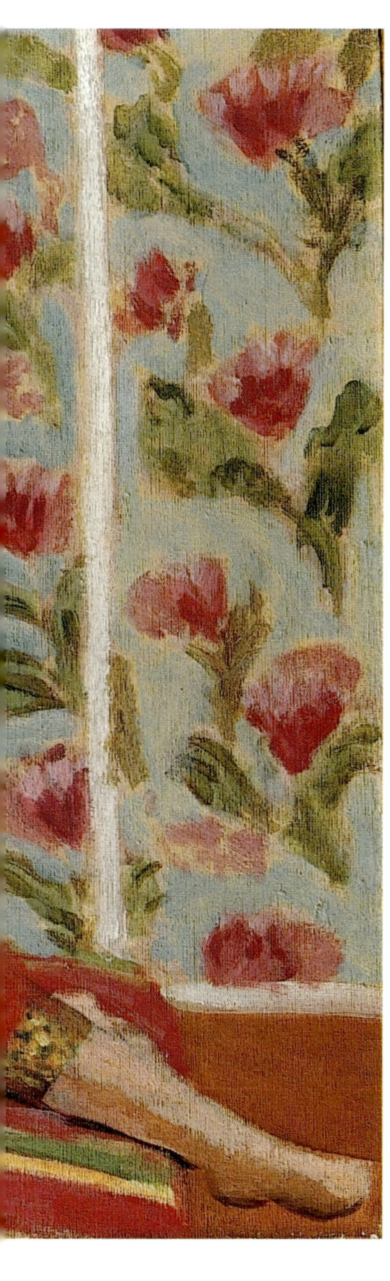

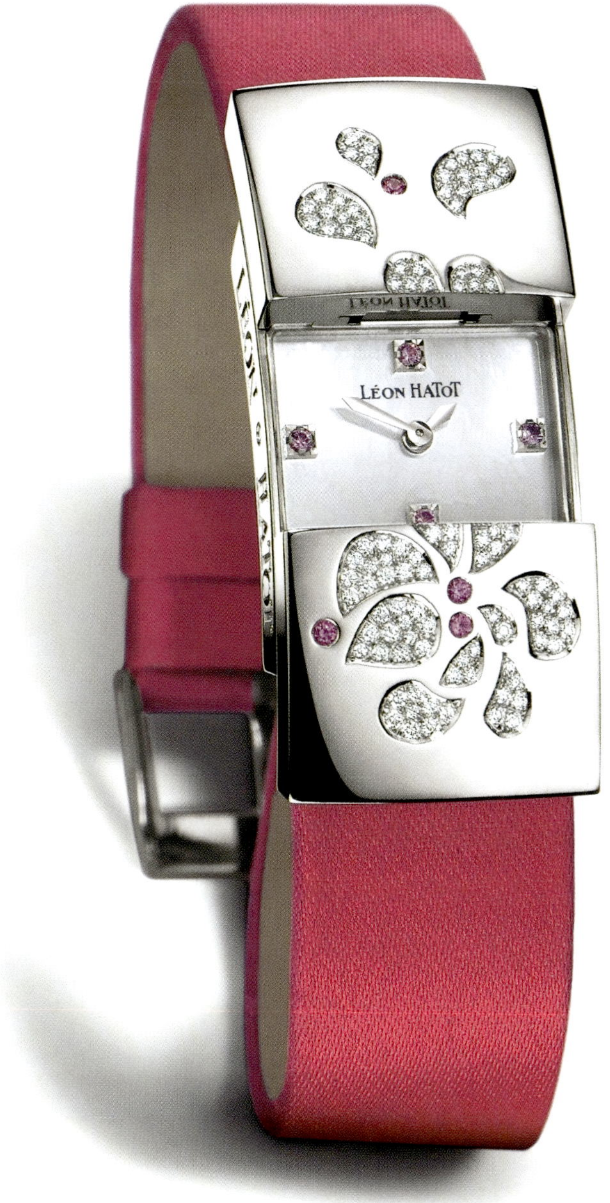

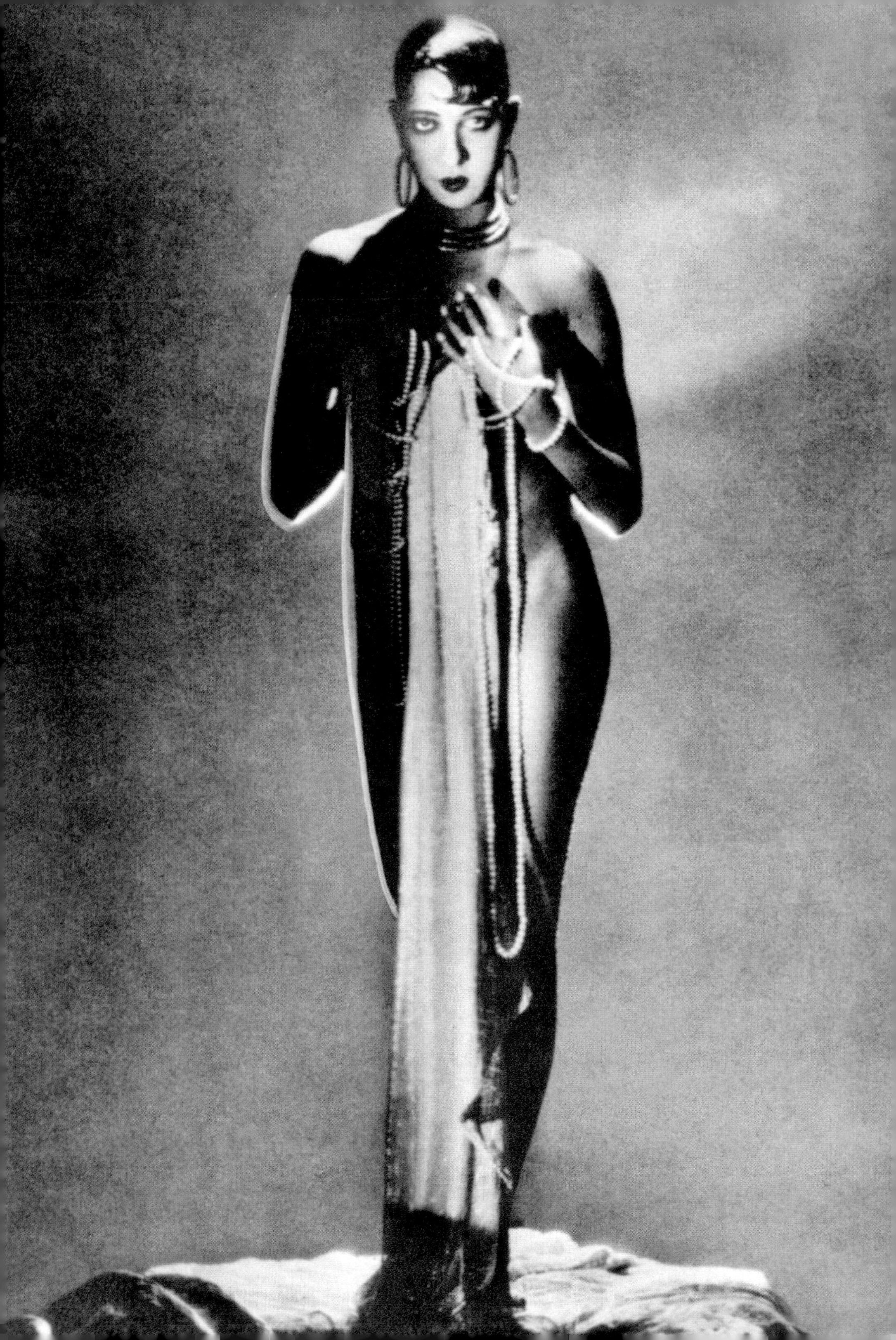

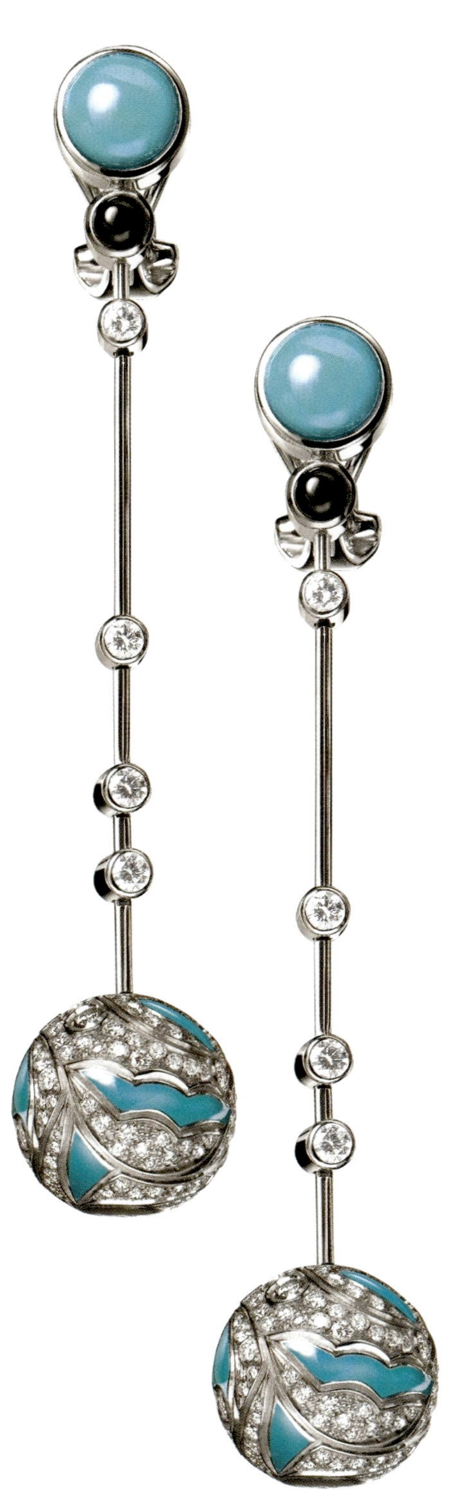

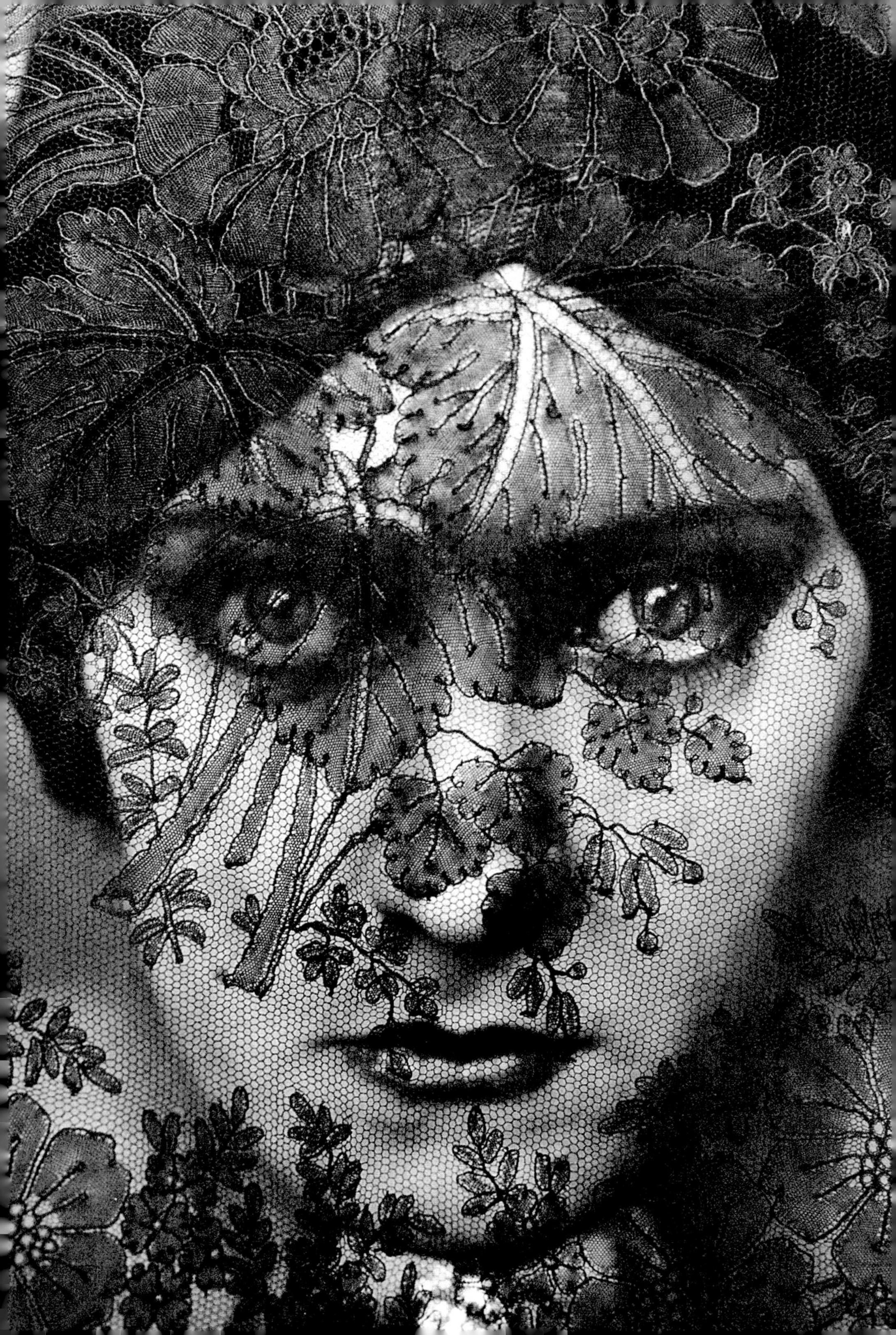

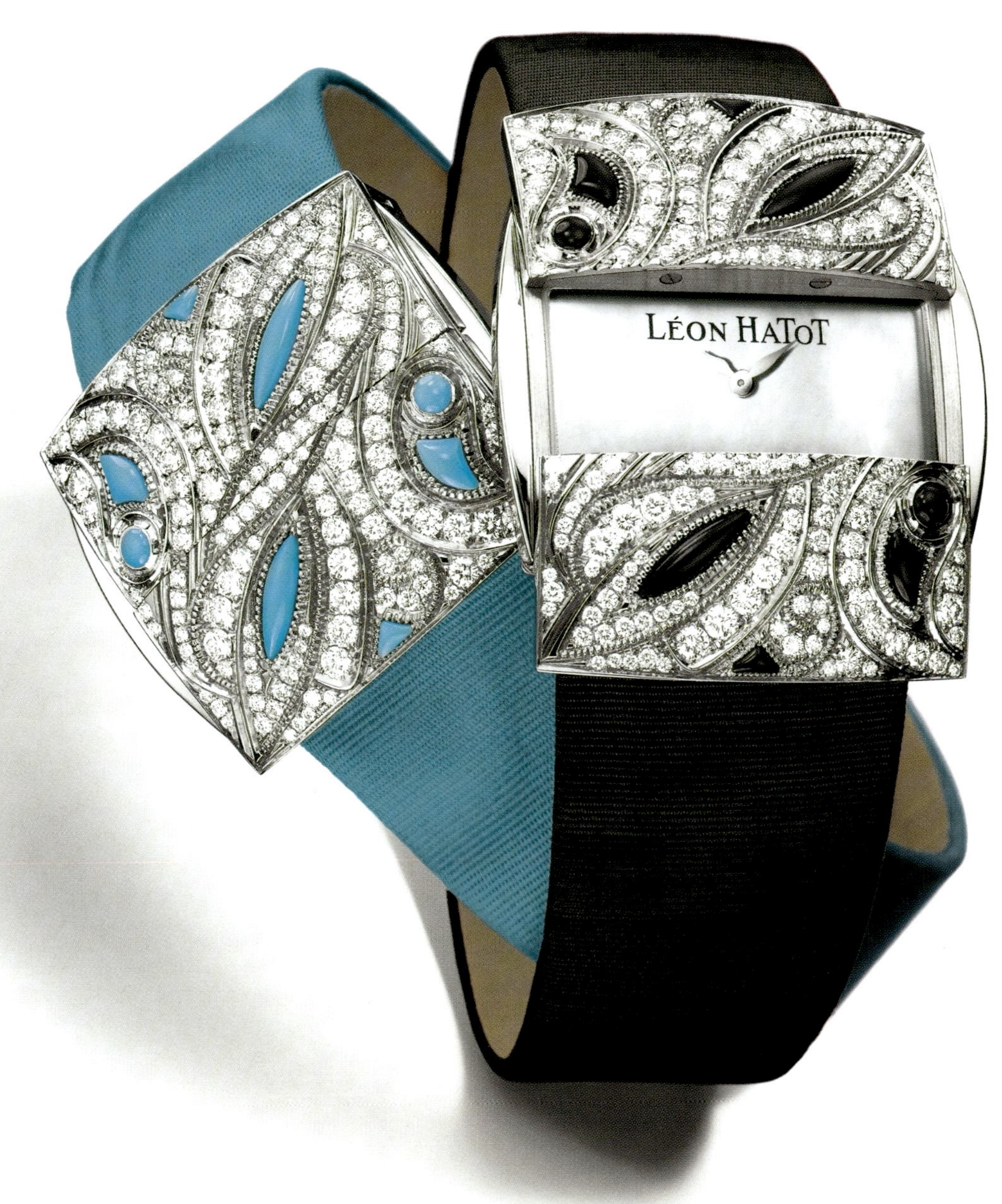

LÉON HATOT

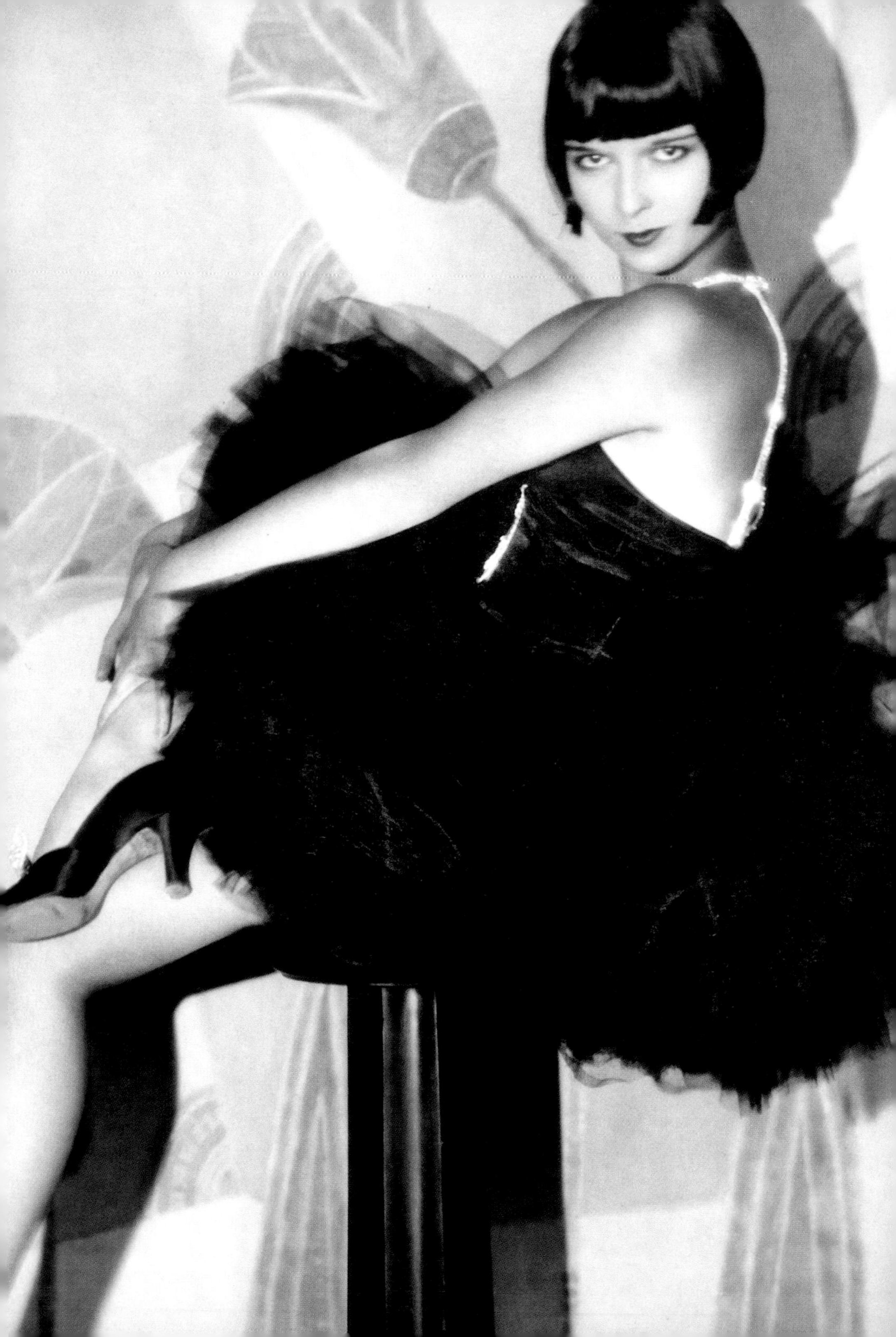

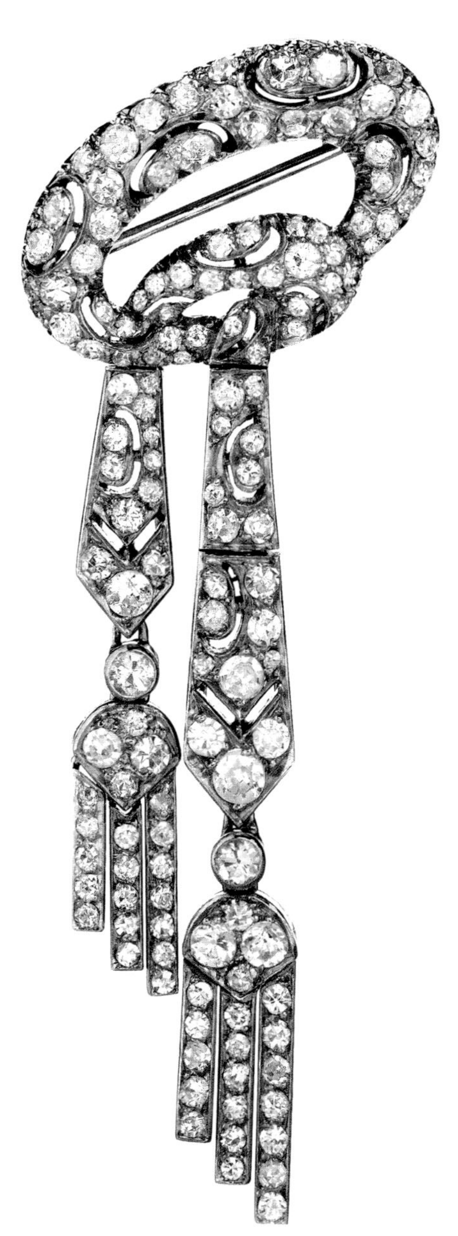

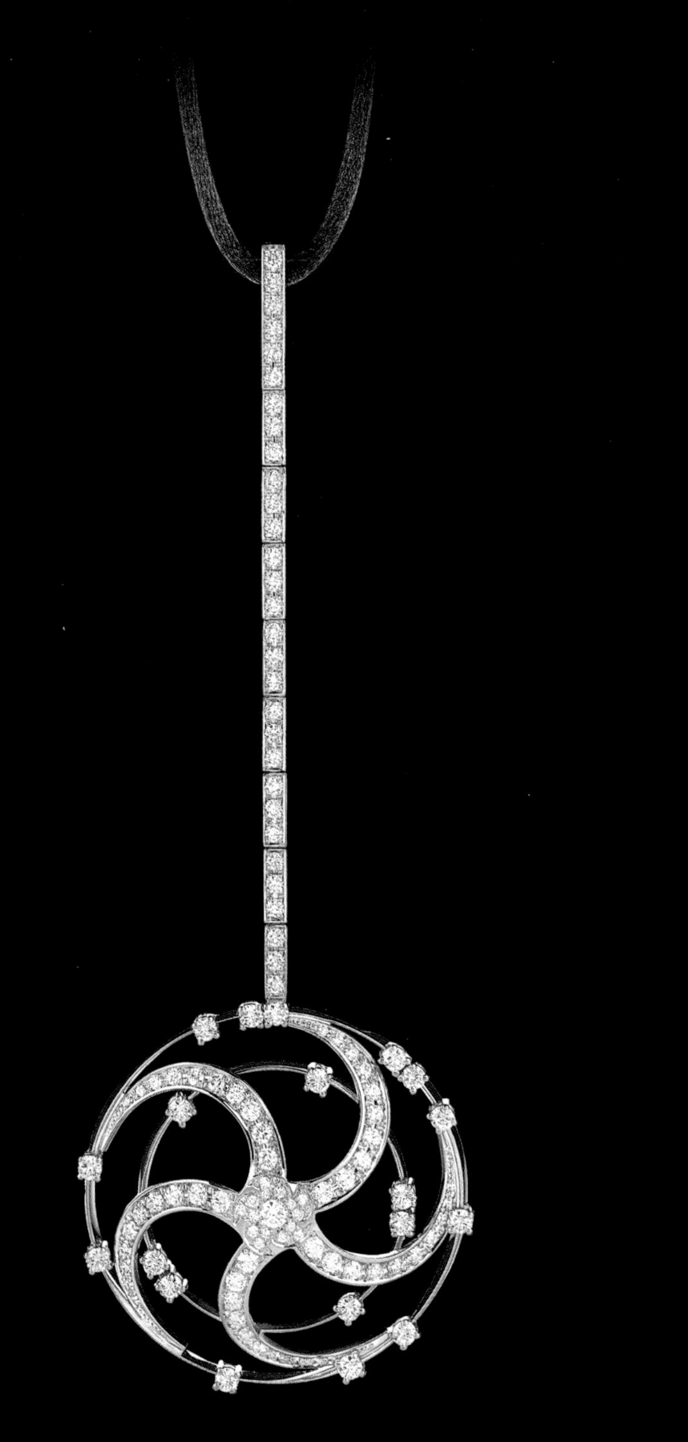

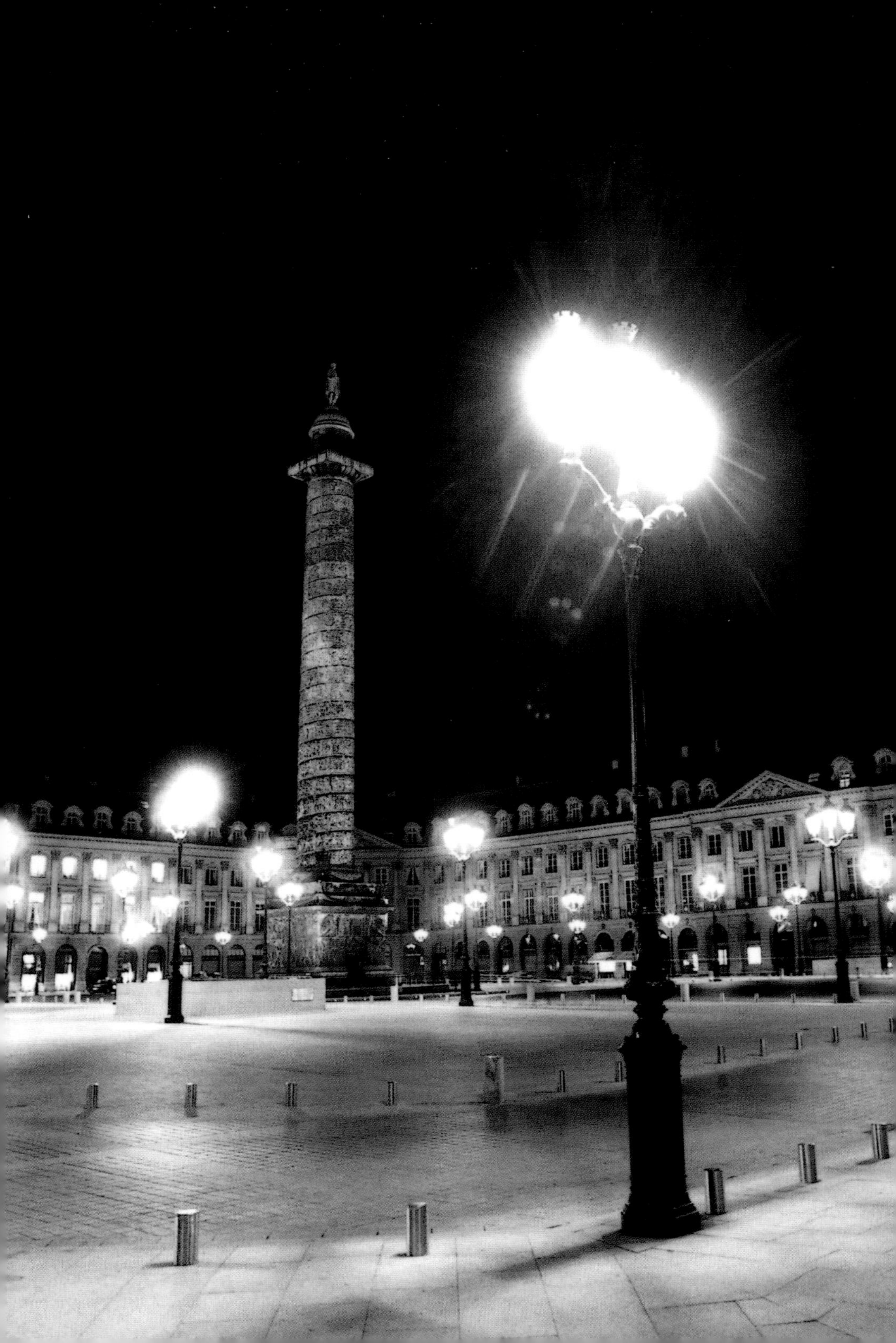

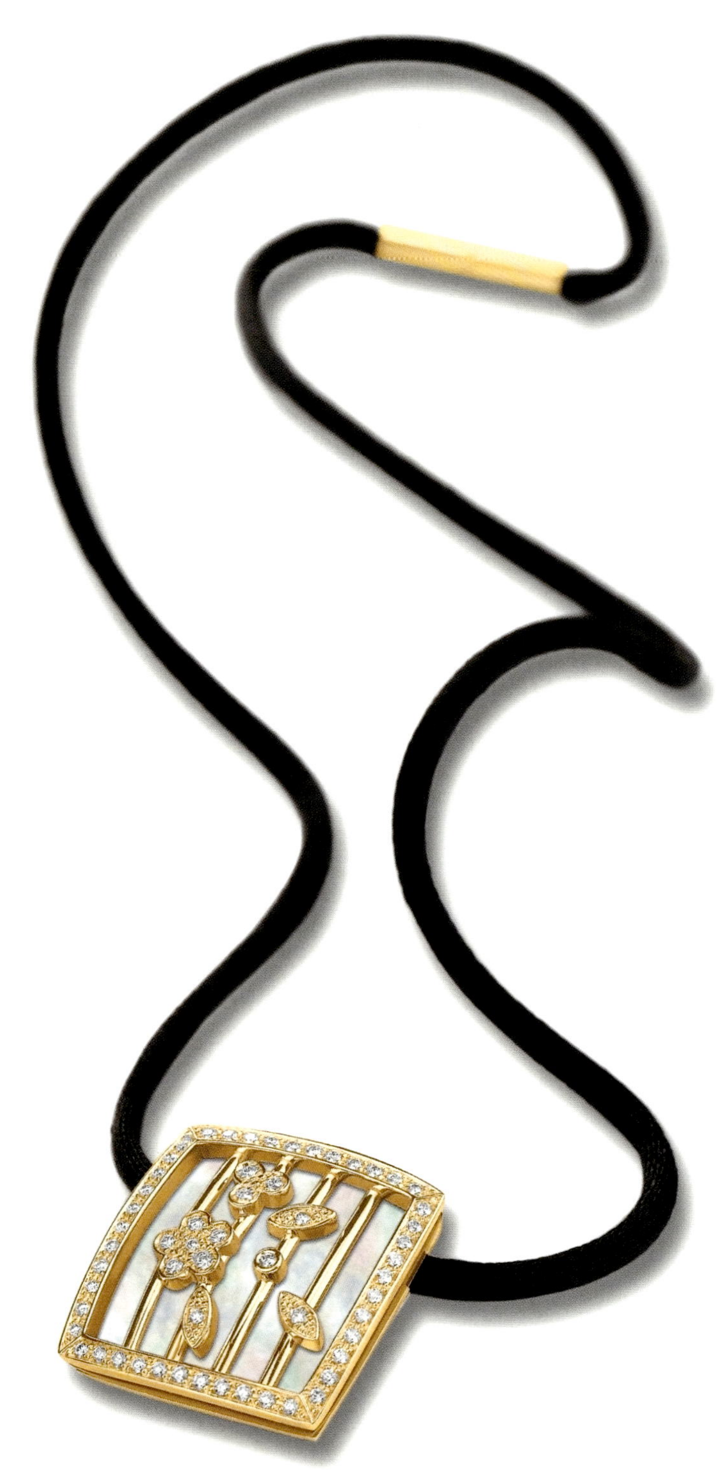

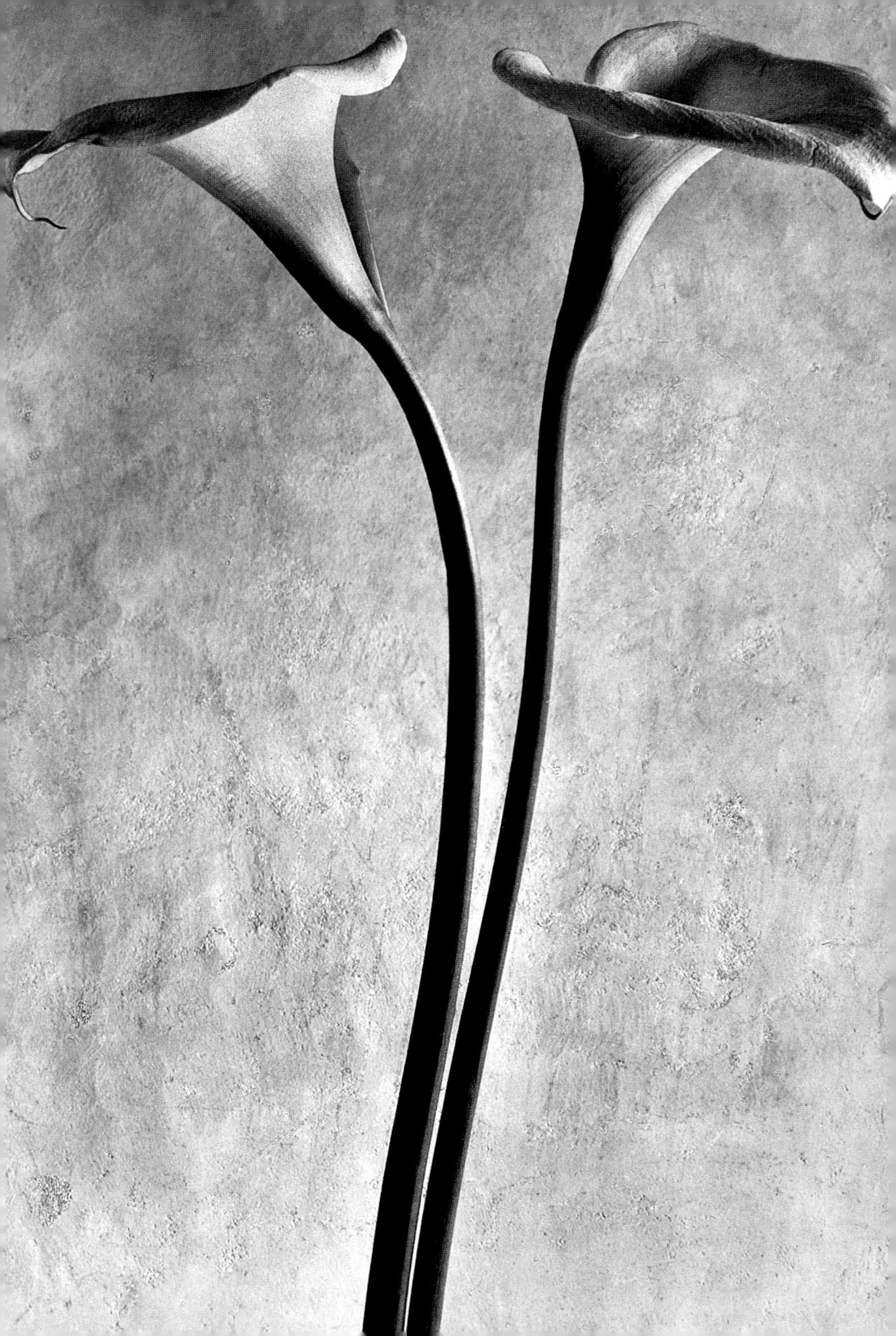

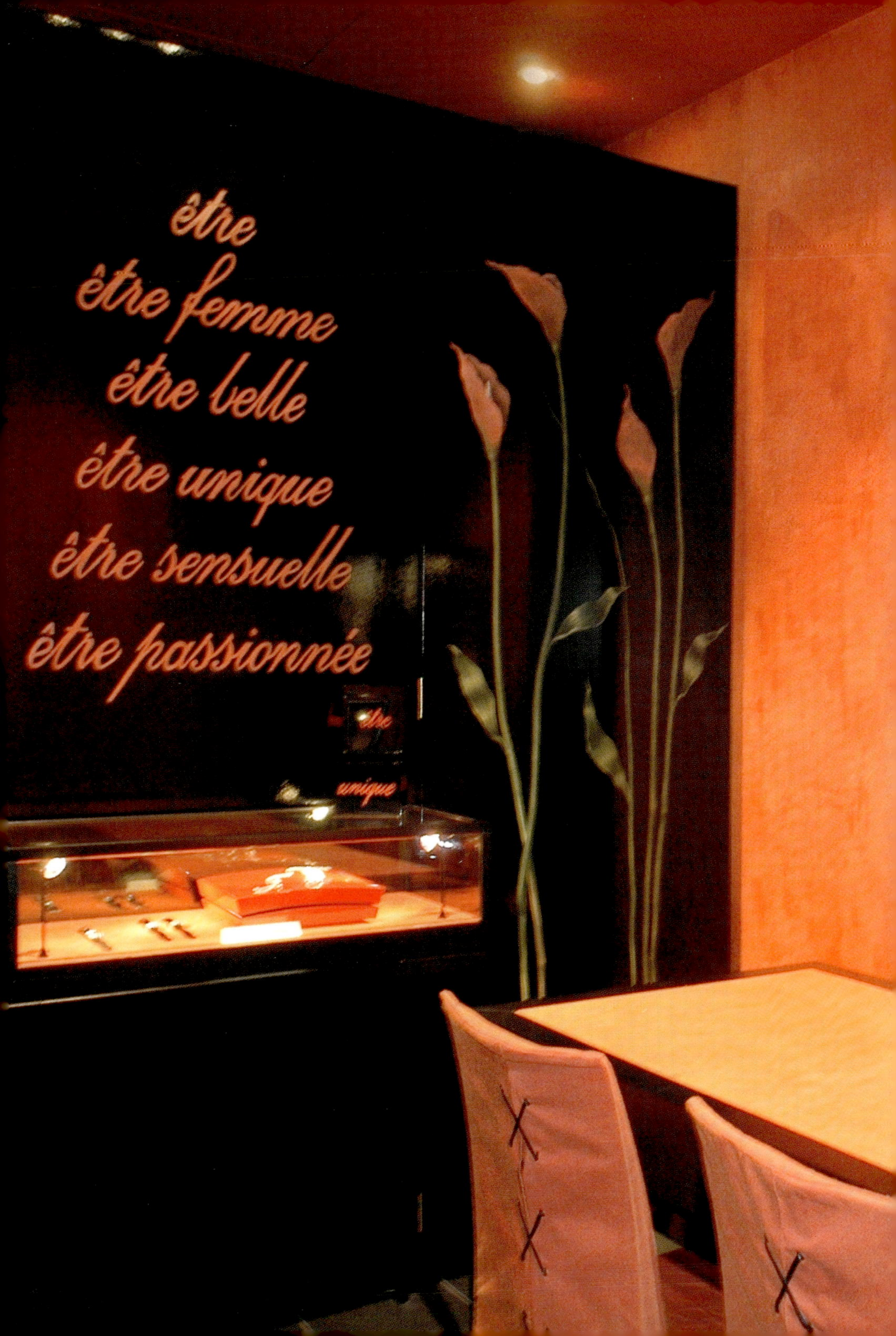
être
être femme
être belle
être unique
être sensuelle
être passionnée

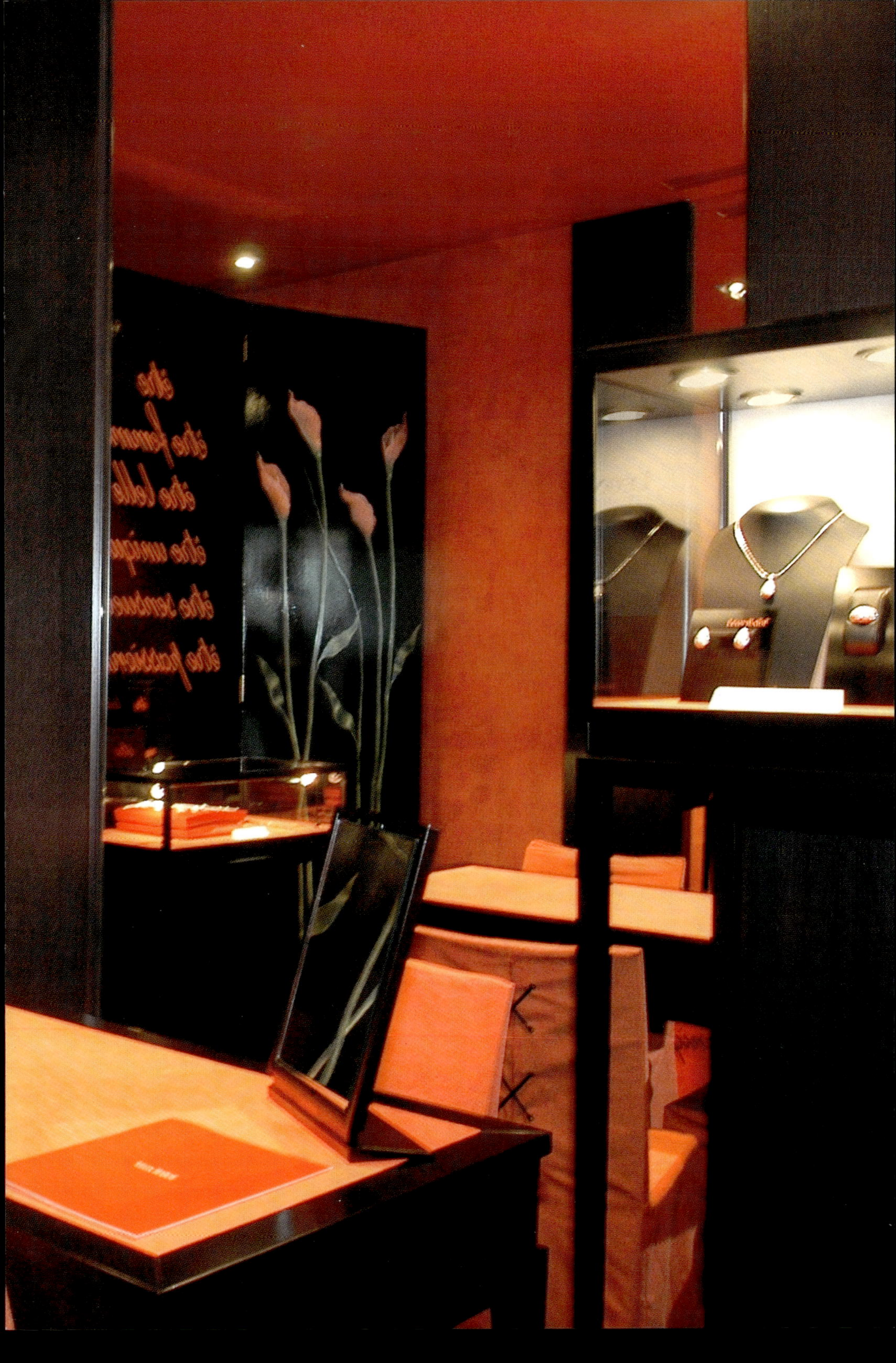

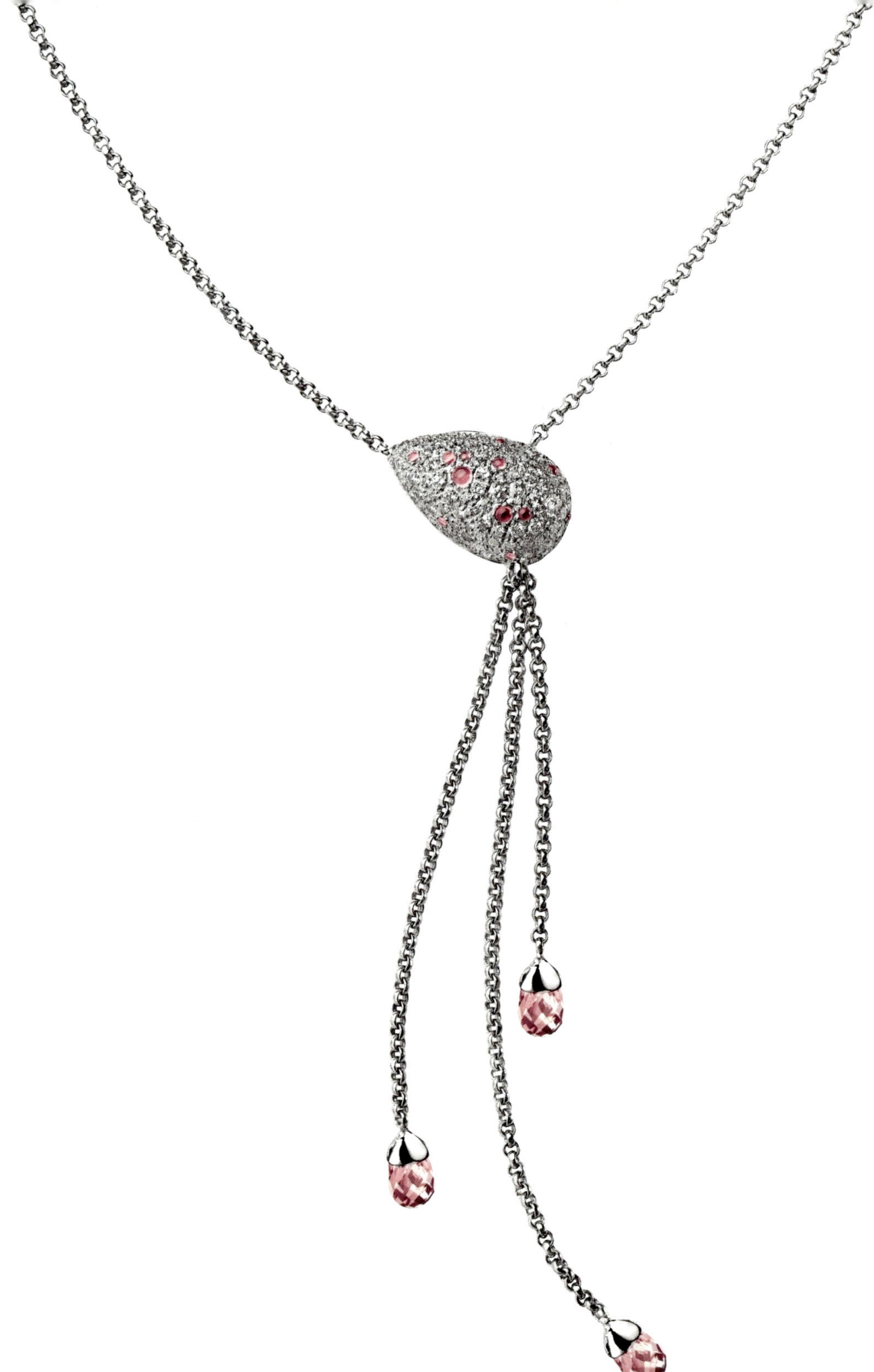

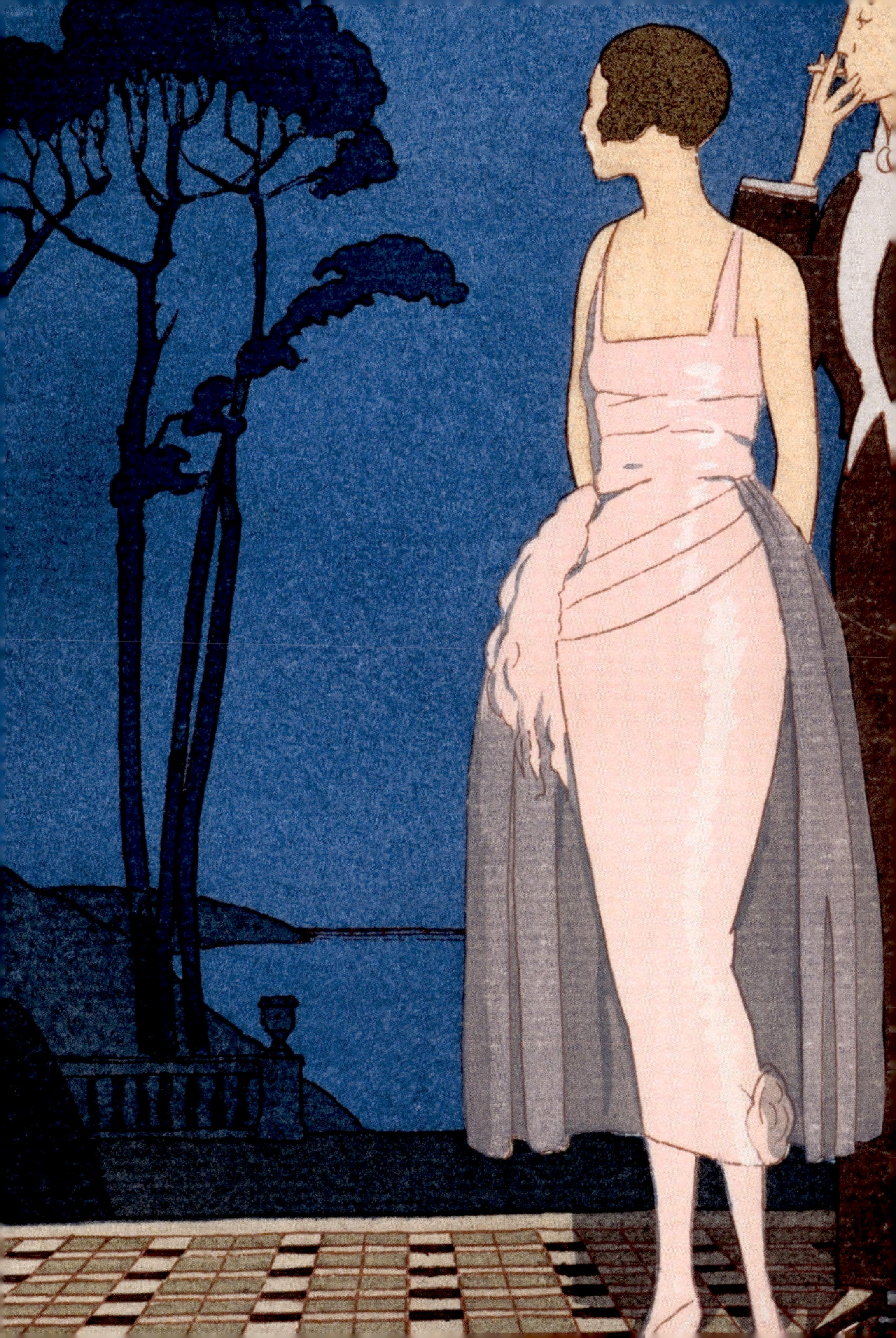

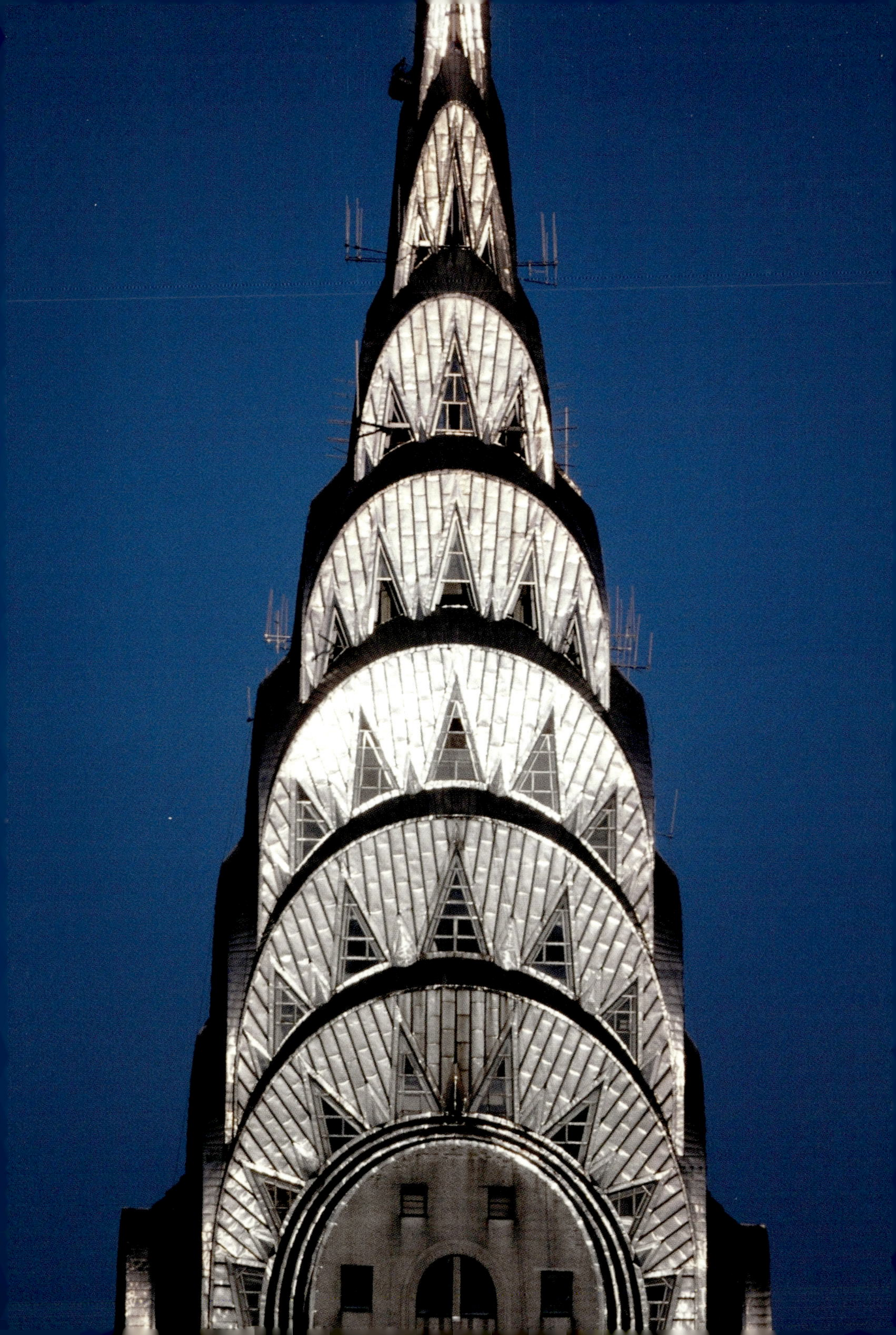

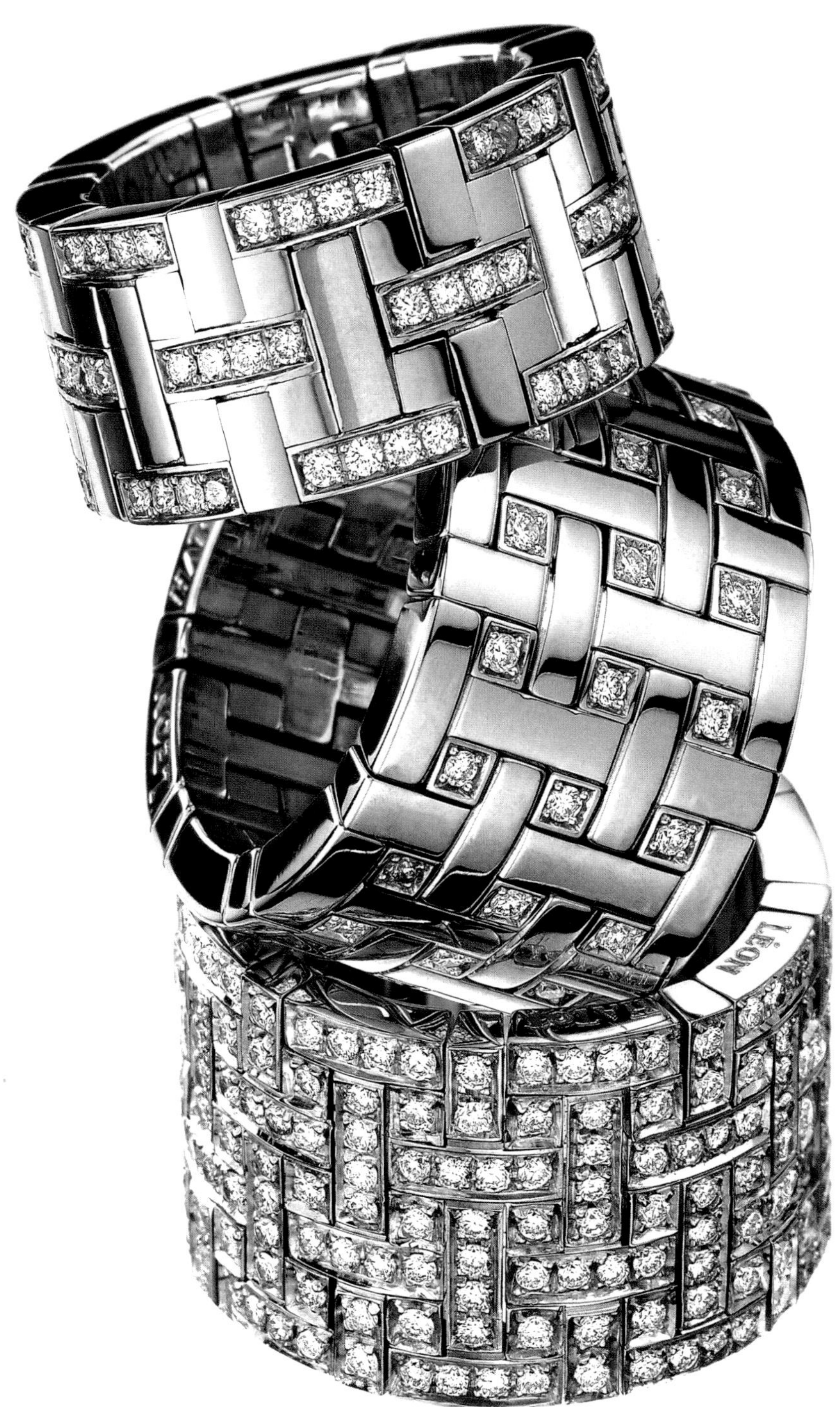

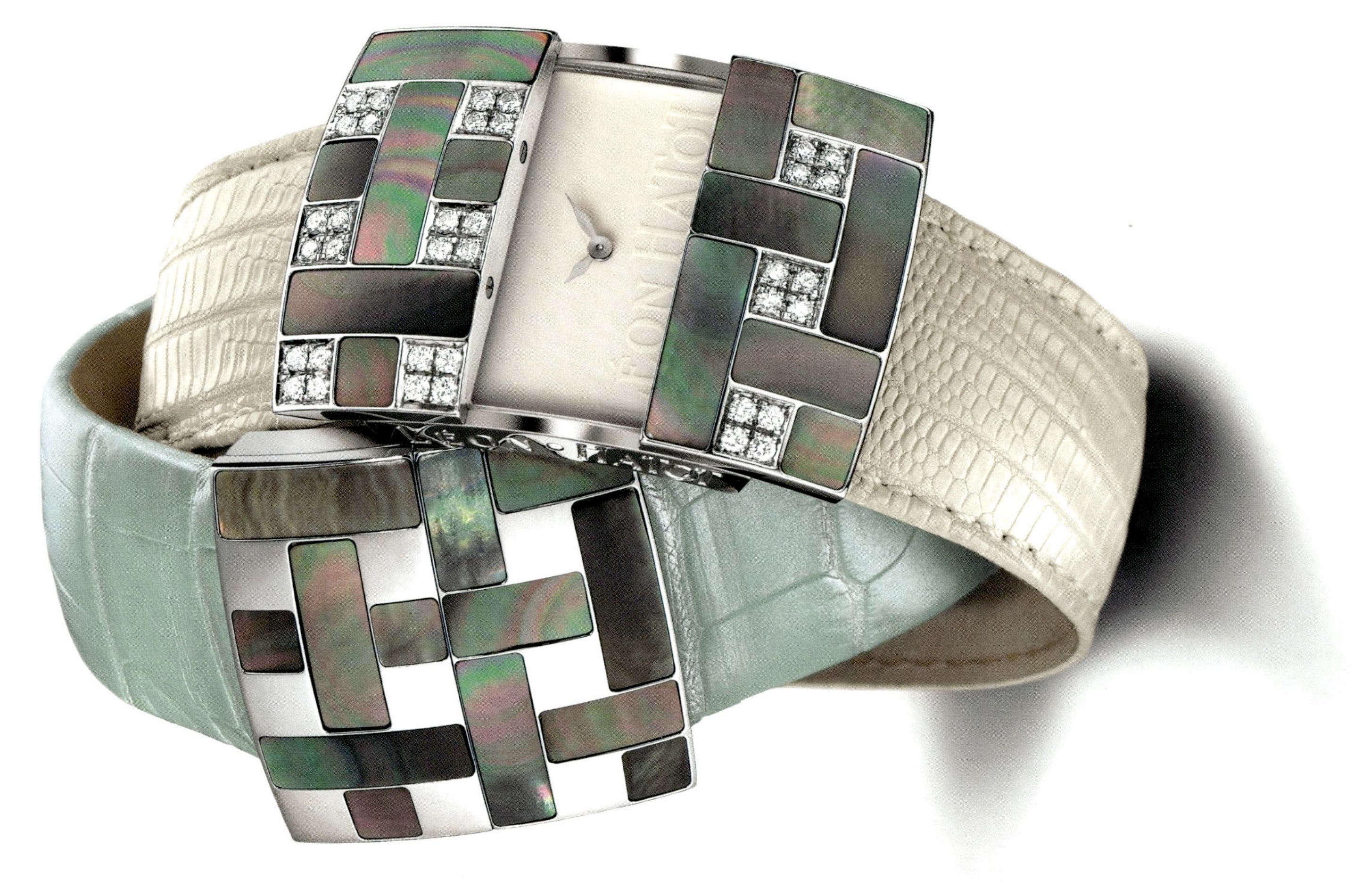
LÉON HATOT

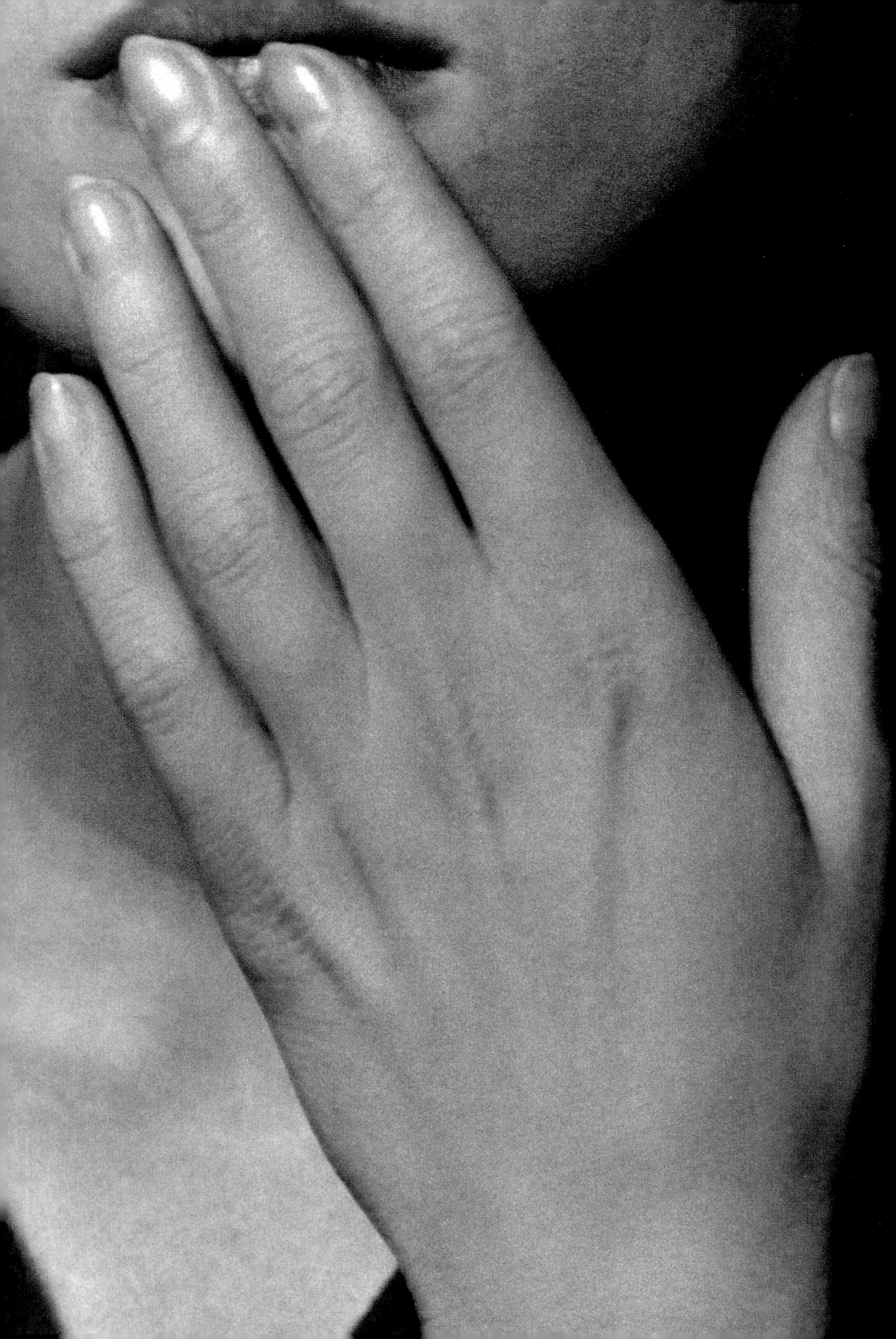

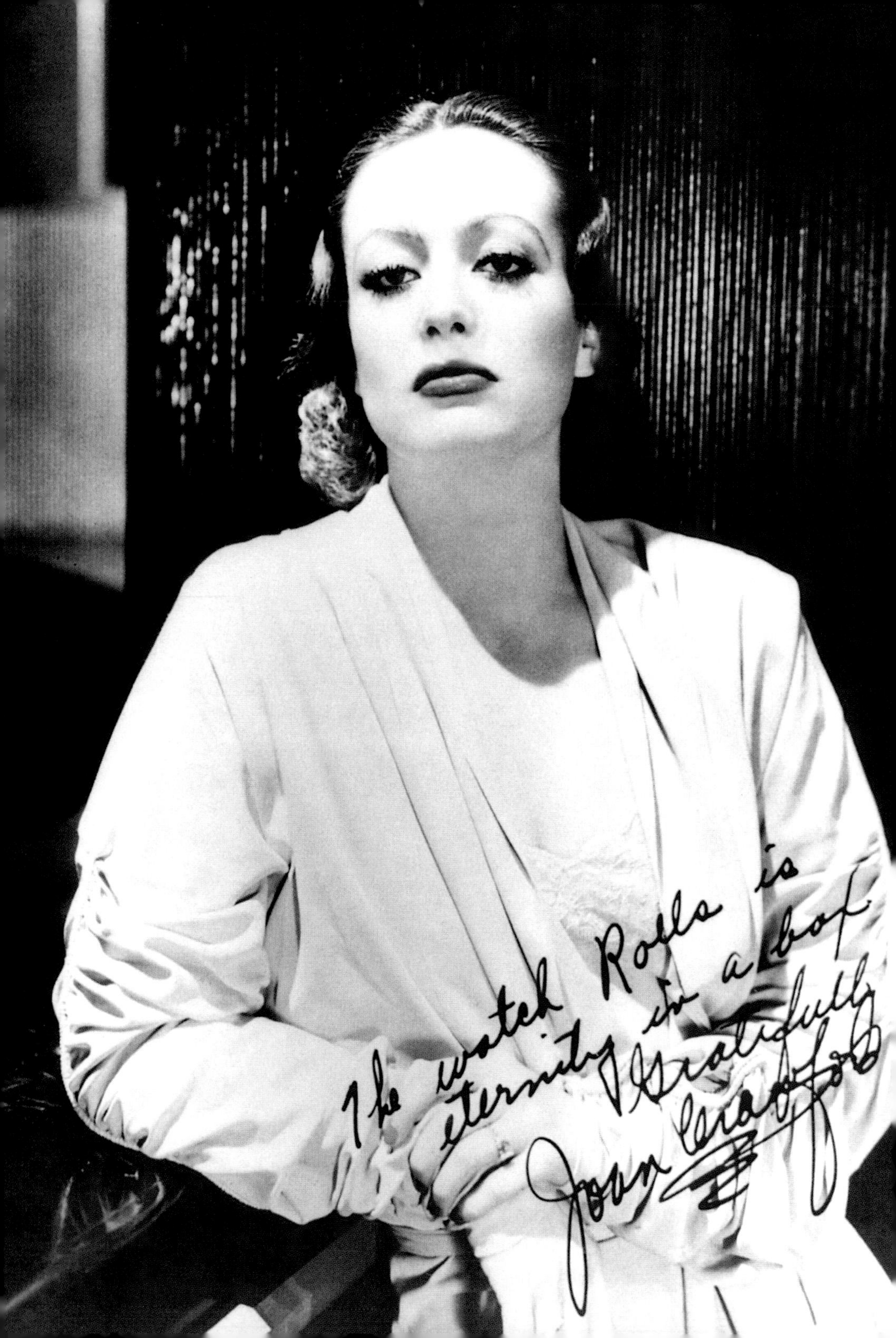
The watch Rolls is
eternity in a box
Gratefully
Joan Crawford

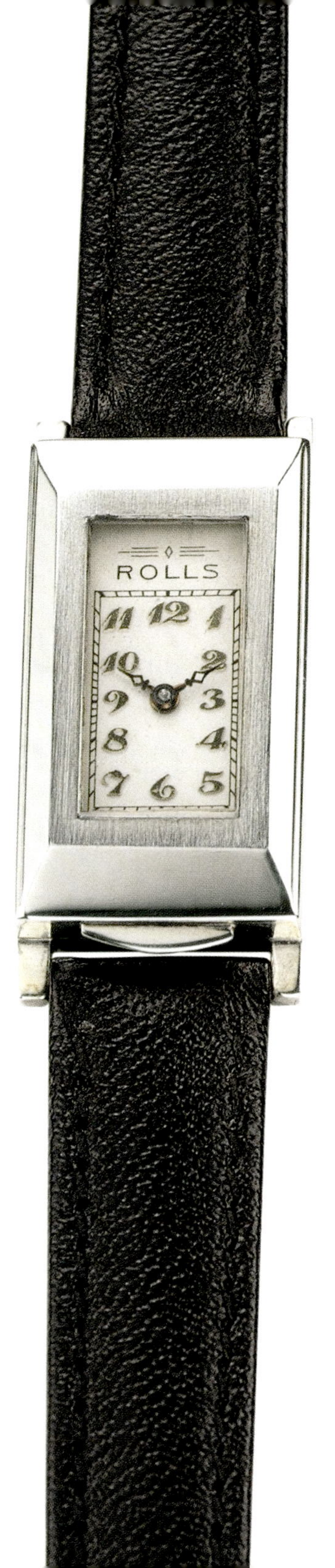
ROLLS

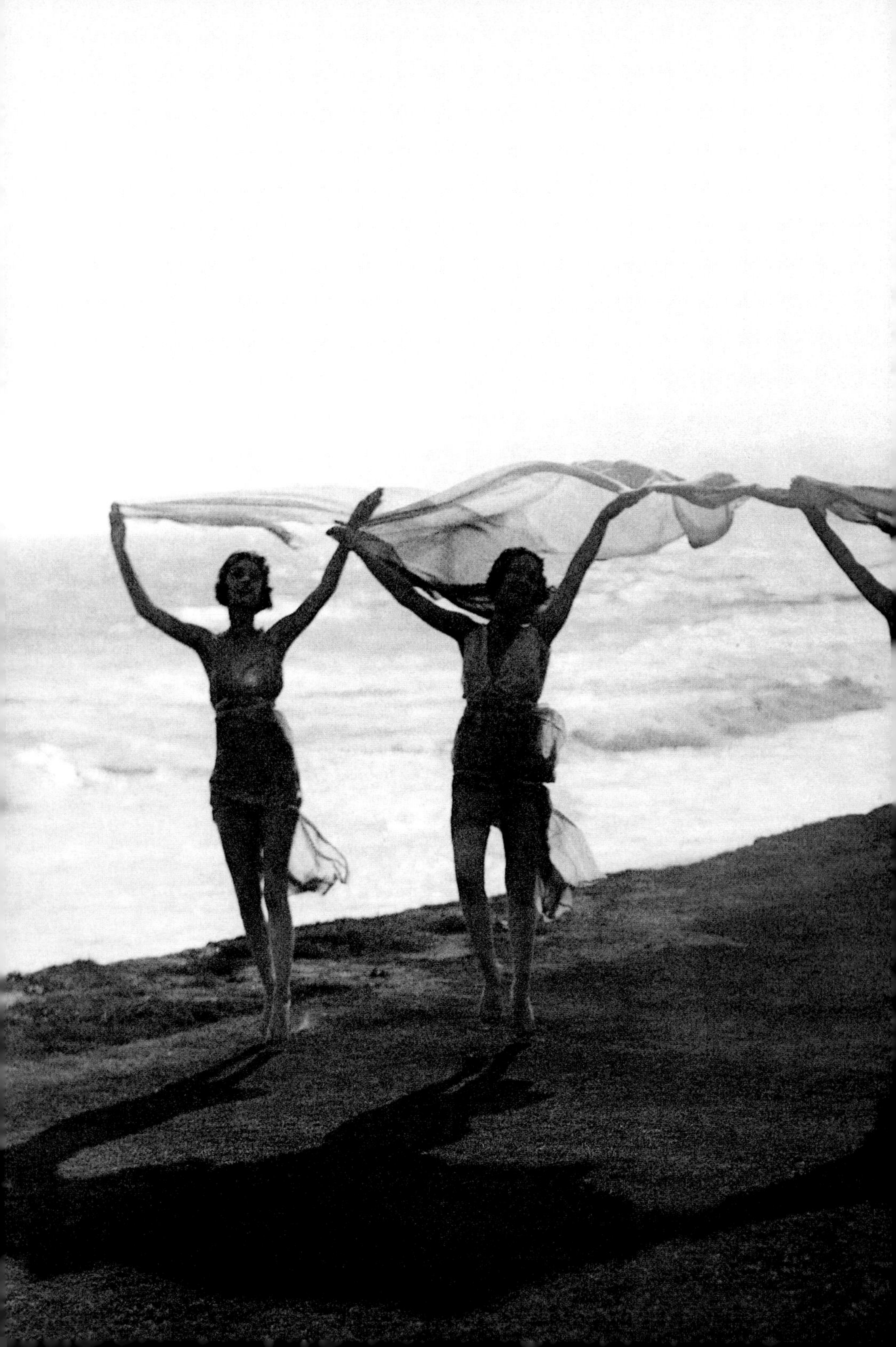

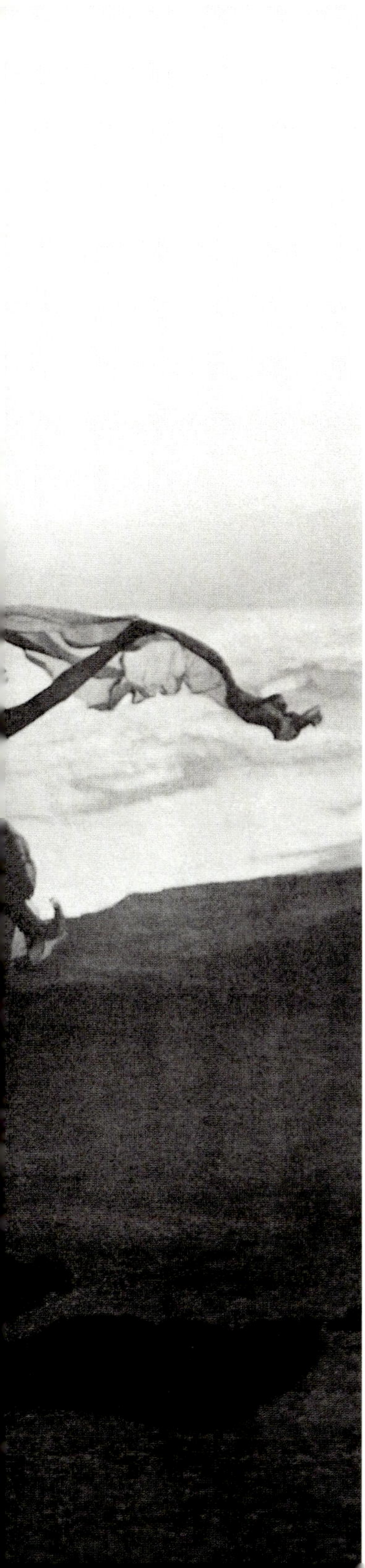

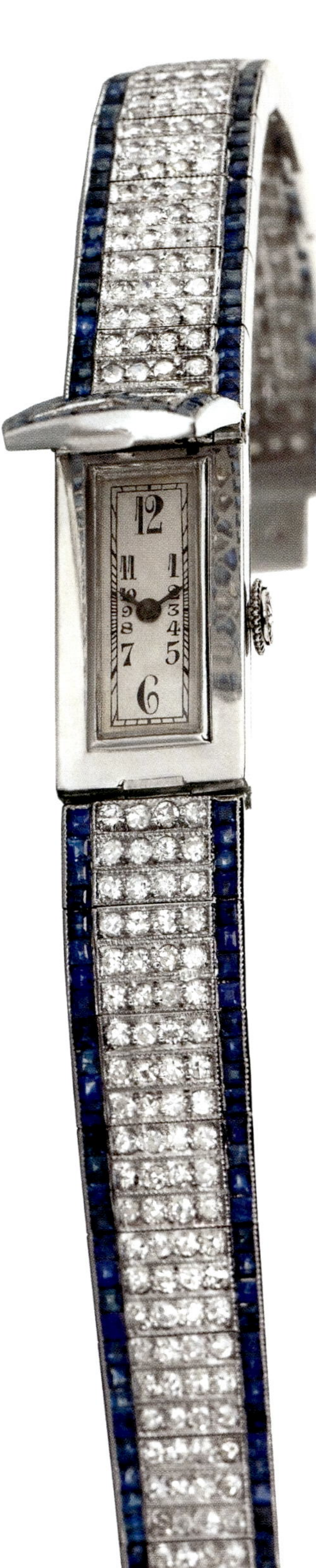

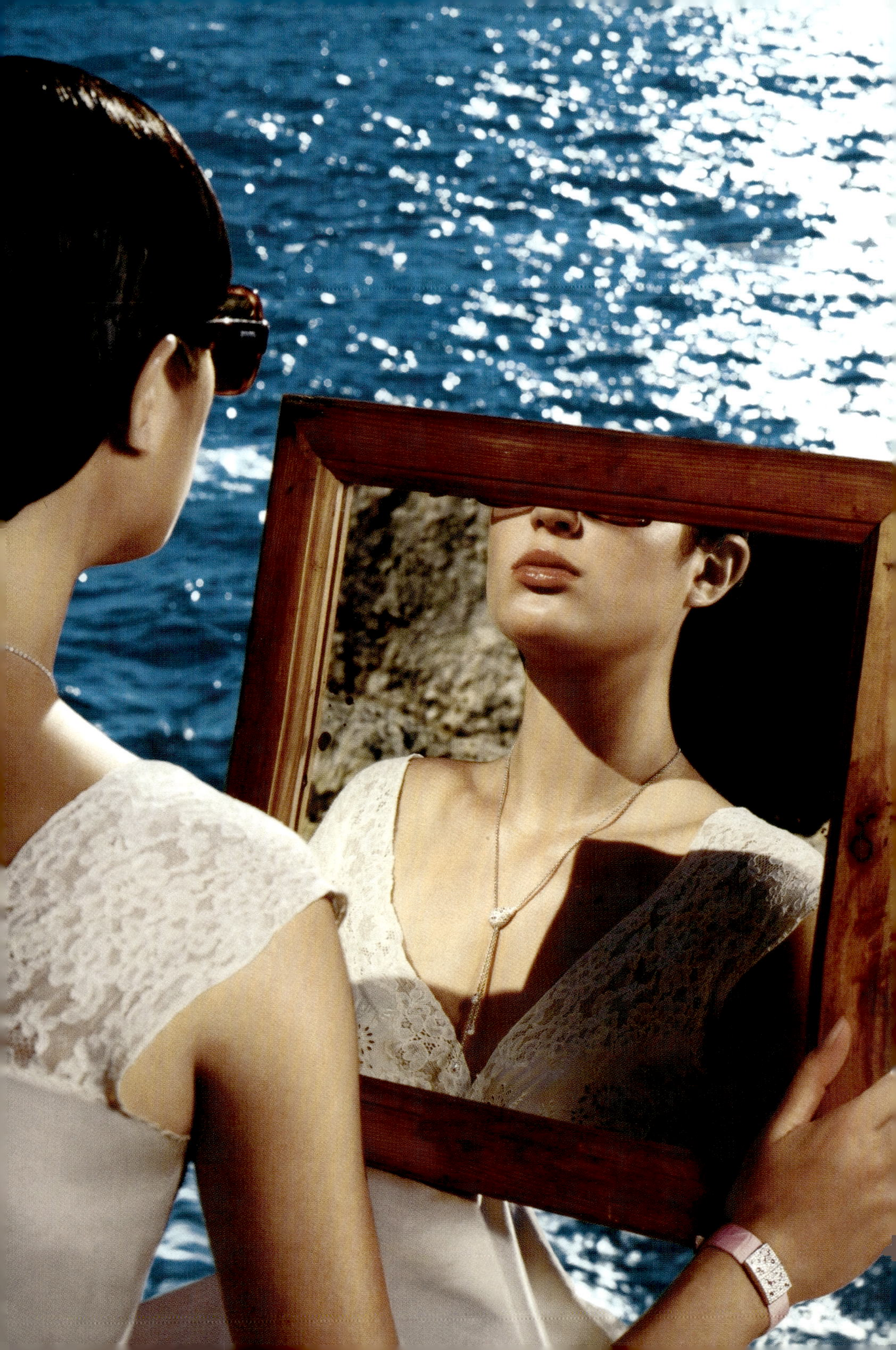

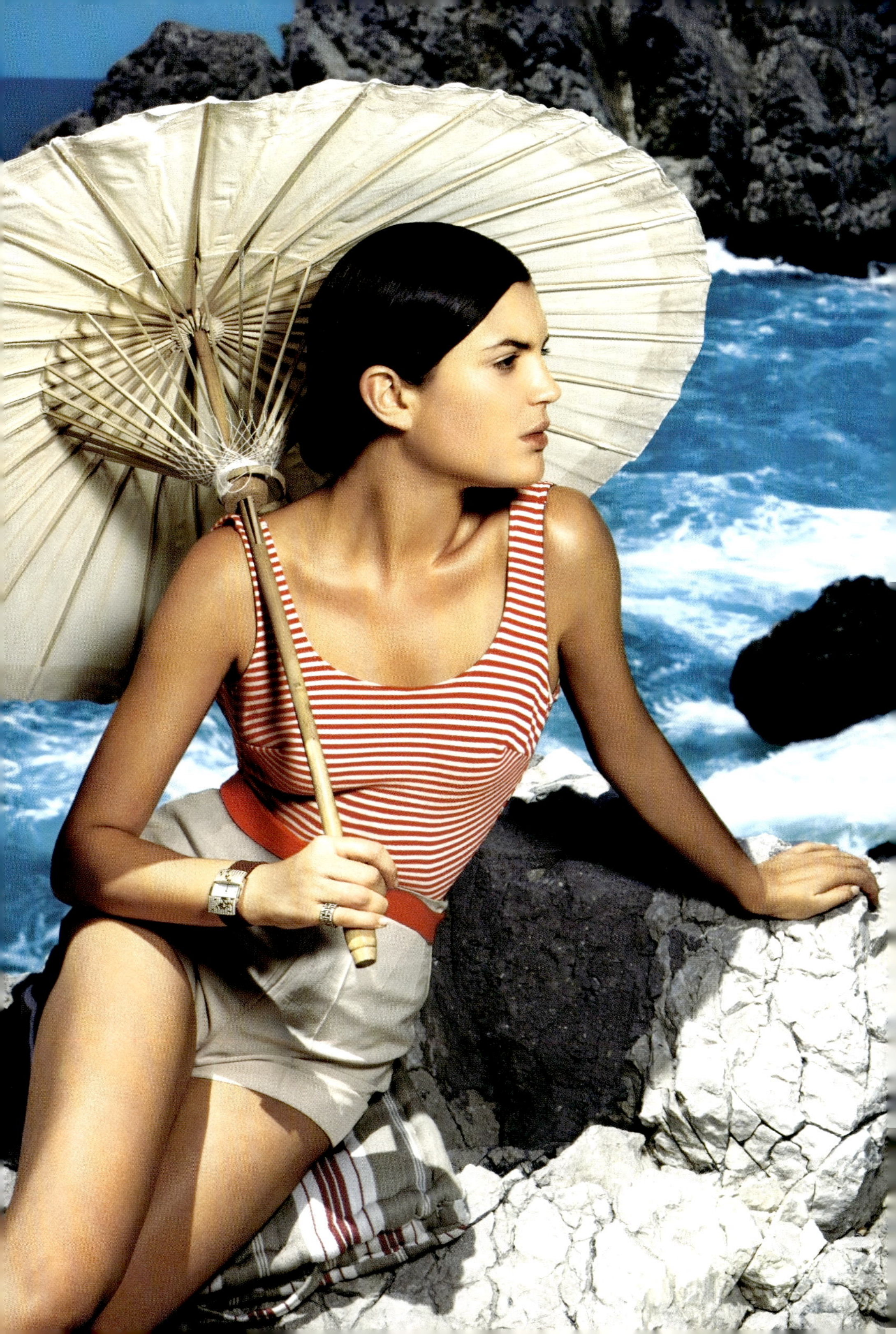

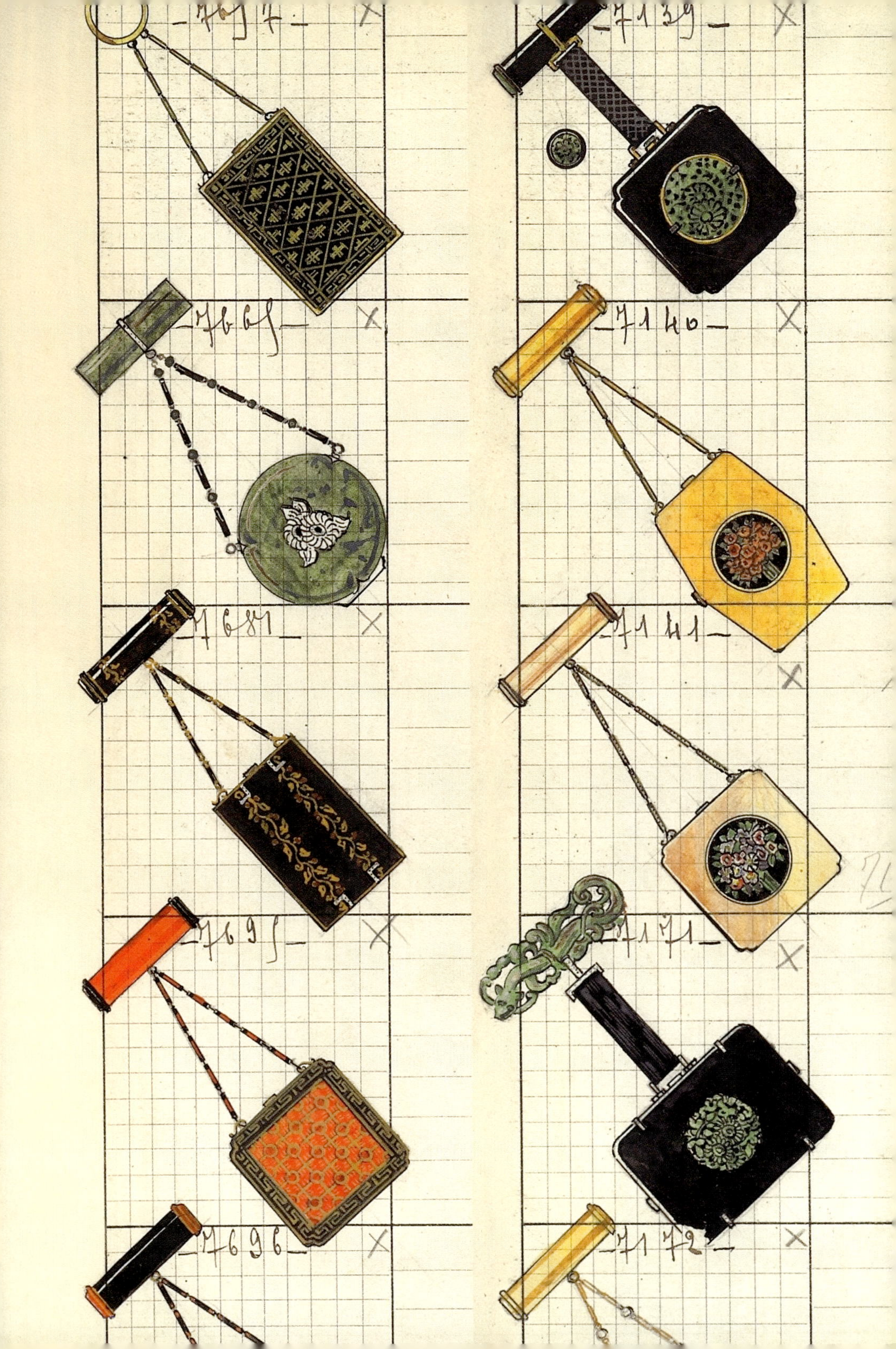
7137
7139
7669
7140
7687
7141
7695
7171
7696
7172

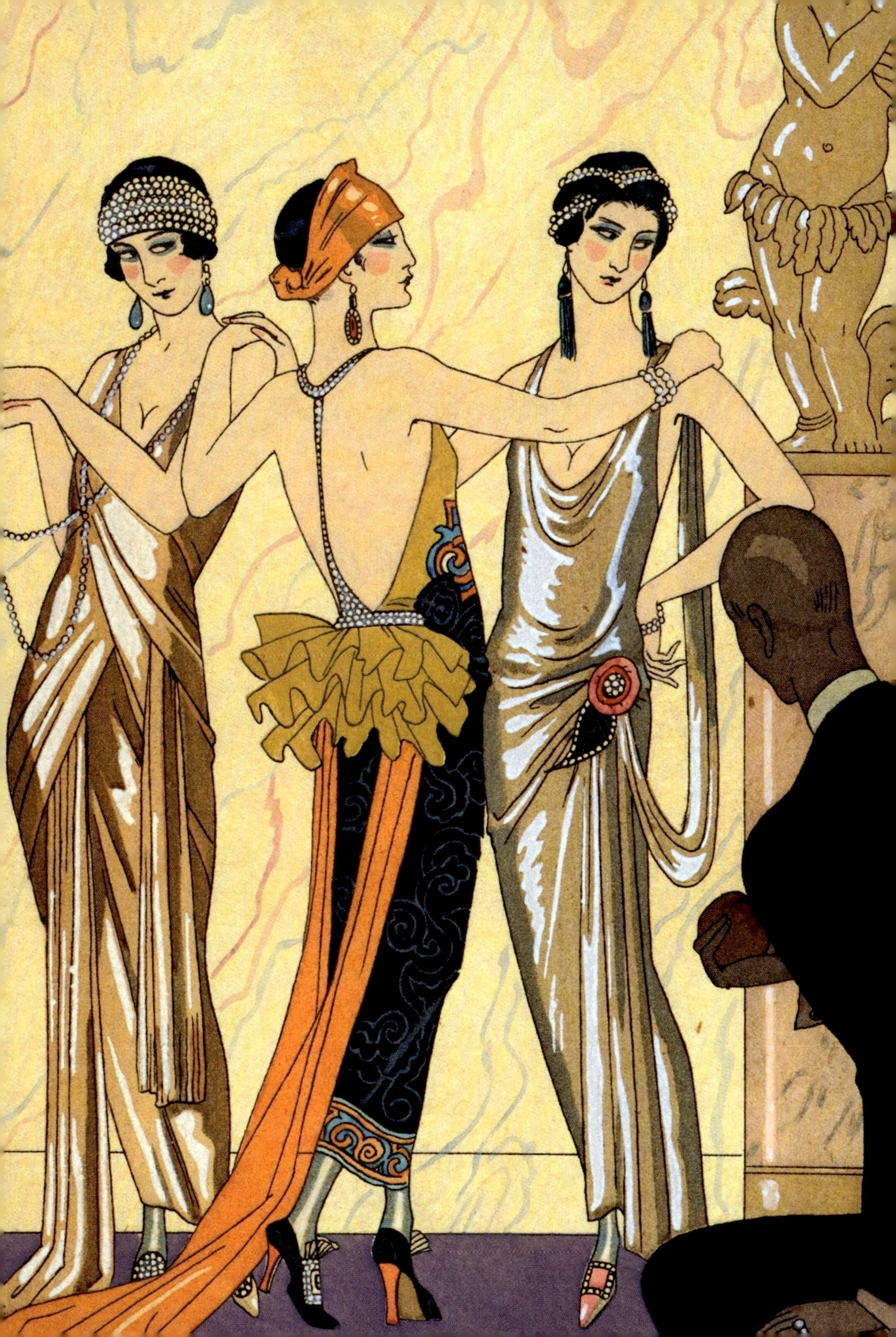

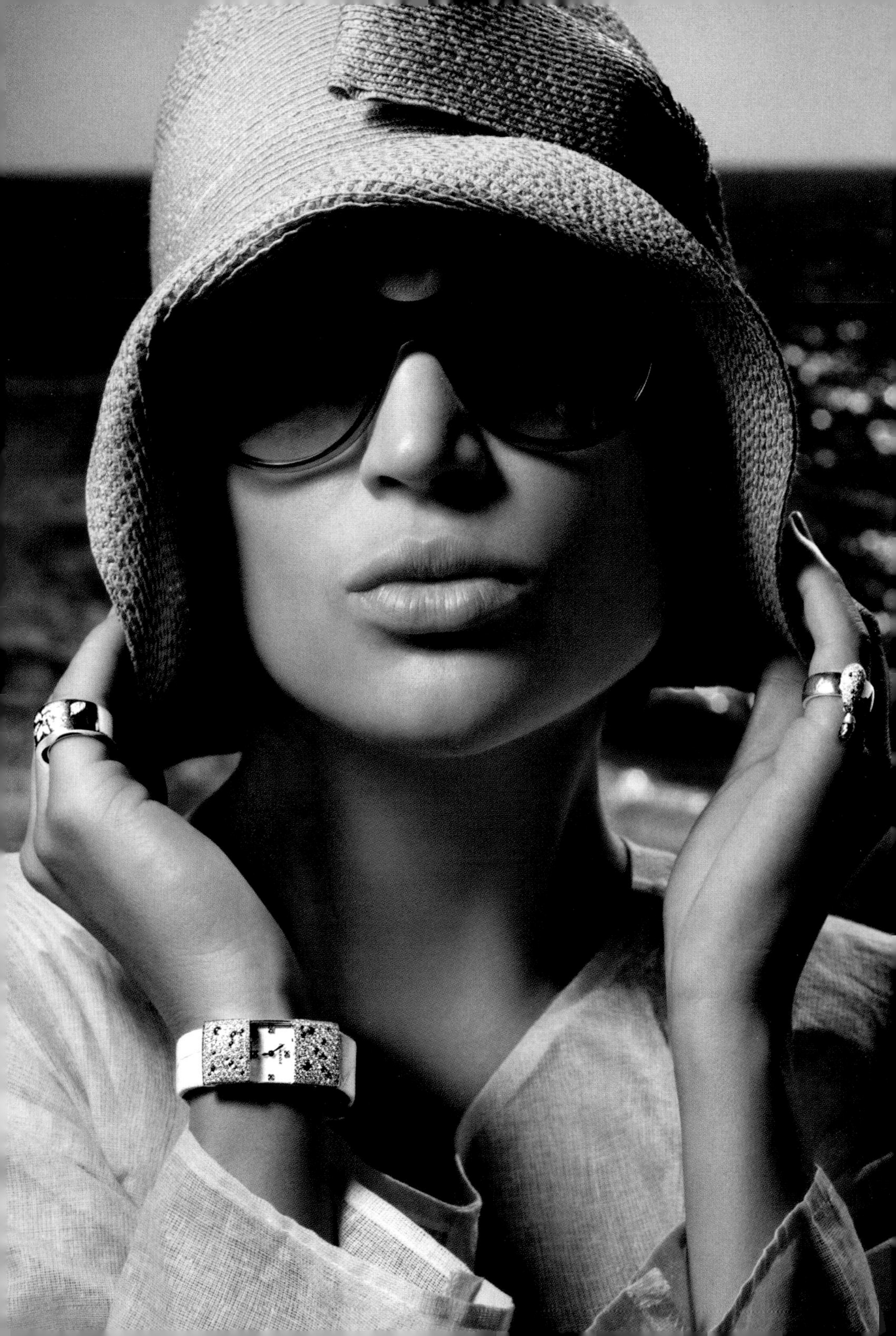

Chronology

1883: Léon Hatot was born on April 22nd in Châtillon-sur-Seine, in Burgundy.

1895: He studied watchmaking then, after 1898, fine arts, at schools in Besançon.

1905: Léon Hatot opened his own workshop, specializing in jewelry, precious metal engraving and quality watches.

1911: He moved to Paris where he took over the watch and jewelry supplier Brédillard, adding the leading names on Rue de la Paix and Place Vendôme to his clientele.
The City of Besançon commissioned the young watchmaker and jeweler to create a hunter watch as a gift for President Armand Fallières on an official visit to the region.

1914: Léon Hatot enlisted in the forces and distinguished himself with the invention of a cost-effective process to manufacture mechanical artillery parts.

1919: With peacetime, the Hatot workshops returned to the making of luxury watches and jewelry.

1920: Léon Hatot set up a subsidiary to research and develop battery-driven watches and clocks.
He founded *Société des Établissements Léon Hatot*.
The watch review *La France Horlogère* invited him to join its editorial board, where he was presented as "Hatot Industrialist and Craftsman-Jeweler."

1923: Sales began of "ATO" brand electrical clocks, manufactured in the company's Besançon workshops.
Léon Hatot was made a judge at the Seine commercial court and an advisor to the foreign trade department.

1925: He was awarded a Grand Prix at the International Exhibition of Modern Decorative and Industrial Arts. He was later made a Knight of the Legion of Honor.

1928: Invention of the "Ato-Radiola" electrical clock which used radio waves to automatically set the time.
The company transferred its different workshops to luxurious premises at 12, Rue du Faubourg Saint-Honoré in Paris.

1930: Invention of the "Rolls", a revolutionary self-winding watch that earned Léon Hatot a Medal of Honor from the *Société d'Encouragement pour l'Industrie Nationale*.

1931: Léon Hatot's compact electrical clocks were an acclaimed feature of the Colonial Exhibition. They would inspire a new generation of models whose movement was a decorative element in itself.
A founder-member of the *Société Chronométrique de France*, Léon Hatot was commissioned to design the crystal cup awarded to the winner of the annual chronometry competition.

1933: Léon Hatot acquired Paul Garnier, a company supplying clocks for stations and civic buildings.

1939: The outbreak of war.
The company was assigned production of maritime and aerial navigation instruments.
As from 1940, Léon Hatot refused to carry out any activity that might further the interests of the occupying forces.

1945: The company returned to normal production and contributed to the country's post-war reconstruction. It continued its research activities and filed numerous patents for mechanical, electrical and electronic timepieces.

1953: Léon Hatot, master watchmaker and jeweler, died on September 11th.

1989: On May 10th, Christie's Geneva auctioned a stock of Hatot watches and jewelry that had been locked in a bank vault since 1939.

1999: The Léon Hatot brand was acquired by the Swatch Group.

2002: The revival of a prestigious name.

2003: Inauguration, on December 8th, of the Léon Hatot boutique at 7, Rue de la Paix in Paris.

2004: Inauguration, on May 8th, of a boutique on the Croisette in Cannes.

2005: The one-hundredth anniversary of the brand.

"Coup de Foudre Éclat du Soir" necklace in diamonds and white gold.
A thousand diamonds come together in a dazzling lightning flash. © Jon Compson for l'Officiel, *Paris.*

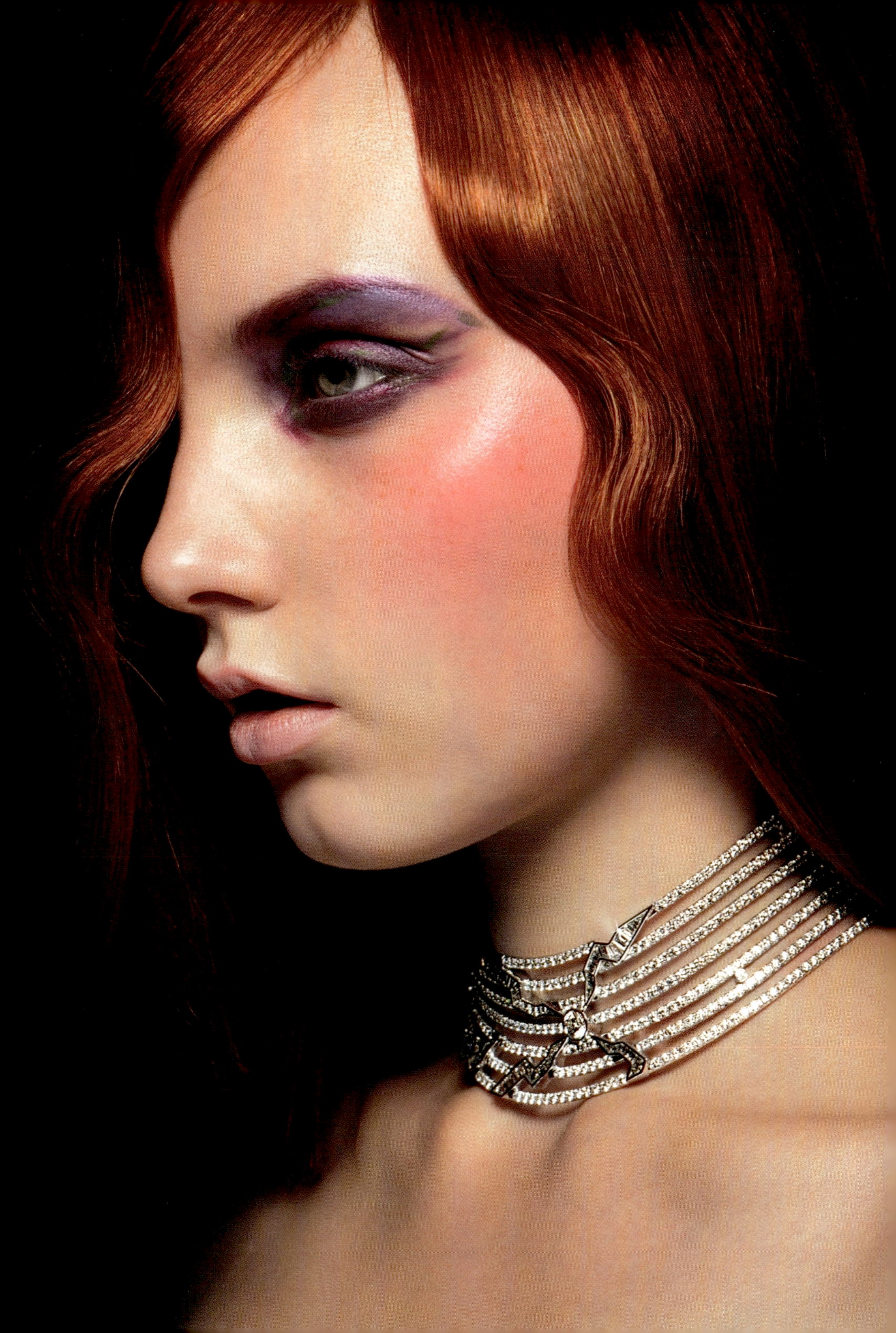

Léon Hatot

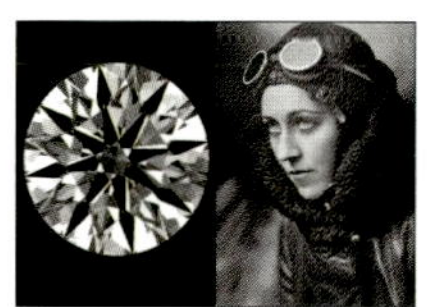

The "Coup de Foudre®" ("love at first sight") diamond is a brilliant which, depending on the angle from which it is seen, reveals eight arrows or eight hearts. Like an invisible signature, it is part of every Léon Hatot contemporary creation. © Courtesy Léon Hatot Archives. **Amy Johnson,** circa 1933-1935. Women played their part in the conquest of the sky. Dubbed Queen of the Air, the record-breaking airwoman Amy Johnson (1903-1941) rose to countless challenges. © Capstack Portrait Archive.

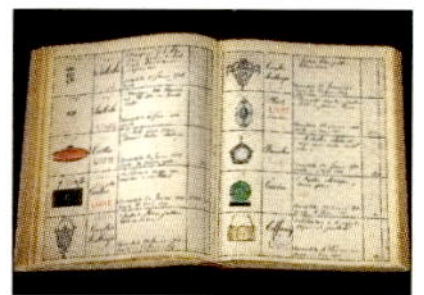

Pages from Léon Hatot's production register for orders placed in early 1914. Watches, jewelry, fashionable accessories and luxury items formed the main of the company's production. © Courtesy Léon Hatot Archives.

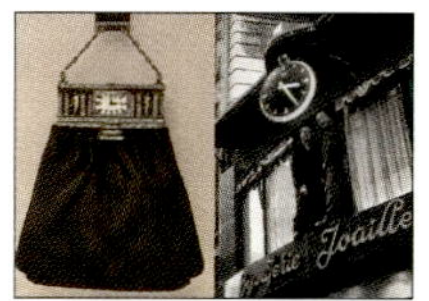

Evening bag in cameos, brilliant-cut diamonds, emeralds, onyx, enamel, platinum and silk grogram, circa 1915. Attentive to an elegant lady's needs, the master jeweler and watchmaker has included a miniature watch in the center of the bag's jeweled clasp. **Curious, creative and inventive, Léon Hatot** (on the left) mastered the art of jewelry and watchmaking to mark his era with his artistic but also scientific creations. © Courtesy Léon Hatot Archives.

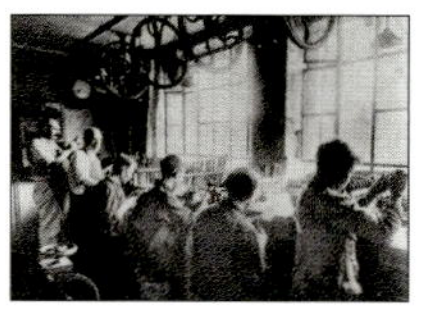

Jewelry workshop. Léon Hatot was still just a young man when he founded his own company in 1905, specializing in jewelry-making and the assembly and finishing of exceptional watches. © Christie's Images.

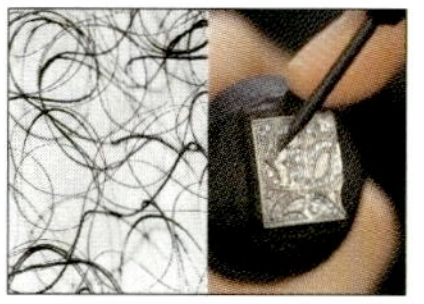

Edward Steichen, *The Wandering Thread,* 1927. The Museum of Modern Art, New York. © Edward Steichen/All Rights Reserved.
Setting diamonds in a dial cover, a canvas on which the stone-setter can demonstrate the full extent of his skill. © Courtesy Léon Hatot Archives.

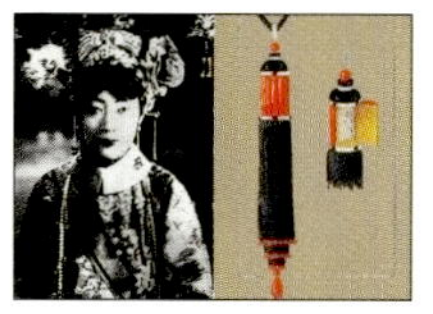

Princess Kuo-Shiasa, China, 1934. China, like Japan, provided Léon Hatot with a wealth of ideas. The jeweler's work is suffused with the subtle imprint of the Far East. © AKG Images Paris.
Project for a pendant watch in coral, onyx, brilliant-cut diamonds, yellow gold and black silk. Original drawing by Léon Hatot in pencil, ink and gouache on cardboard, circa 1925. © Courtesy Léon Hatot Archives.

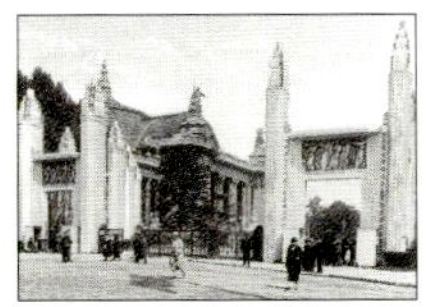

The Porte d'Honneur, one of the monumental entrances to the 1925 International Exhibition of Modern Decorative and Industrial Arts in Paris, where Léon Hatot was awarded a Grand Prix. This exceptional event officially acknowledged the new style to which it would give its name: Art Deco. © Roger-Viollet.

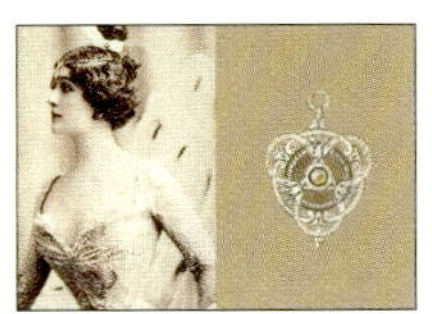

Lina Cavalieri, photographed by Reutlinger in 1908. The voice of this Italian diva (1874-1944), considered one of the world's greatest beauties, lit up the Belle Époque. Private collection. © All Rights Reserved.
Project for a pendant watch in brilliant-cut diamonds and pearls. Original drawing by Léon Hatot in pencil and gouache on cardboard, circa 1905-1910. © Courtesy Léon Hatot Archives.

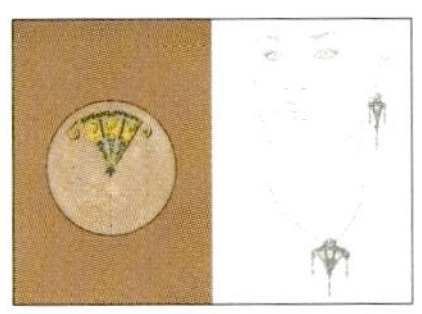

Project for a pocket watch's enamel decoration. Original drawing by Léon Hatot in pencil, ink and gouache on cardboard, circa 1905. © Courtesy Léon Hatot Archives.
Project for a line of jewelry celebrating the one-hundredth anniversary of the company's founding, 2005. © Courtesy Léon Hatot Archives.

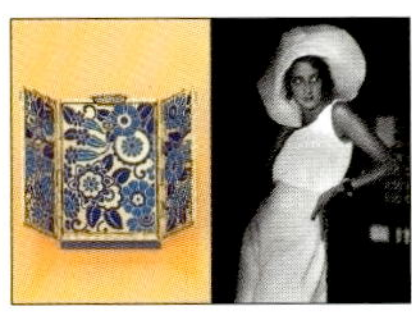

Powder compact in enamel, gold and diamonds, 1928. The compact was popular in the nineteen-twenties among the liberated women who dared to refresh their make-up in public. © Christie's Images.
Renée Perle, immortalized by the loving eye of Jacques-Henri Lartigue. An eternal summer, bathed in light and carefree moments. Biarritz, 1930. © Donation Jacques-Henri Lartigue.

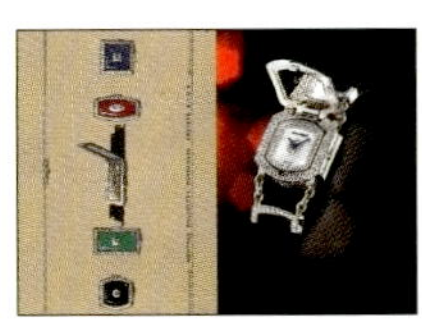

Watches (registered designs), 1922, in platinum and diamonds with a lapis-lazuli, cornelian, jade or onyx center. Gouache on cardboard. **"Éclat du Soir" watch** in white gold, onyx, diamonds, mother-of-pearl and enamel with a watered silk strap. The "stars" of the Roaring Twenties, diamonds and onyx are again united in this precious watch, a contemporary tribute to women, and to Art Deco and one of its uncontested masters, Léon Hatot. © Courtesy Léon Hatot Archives.

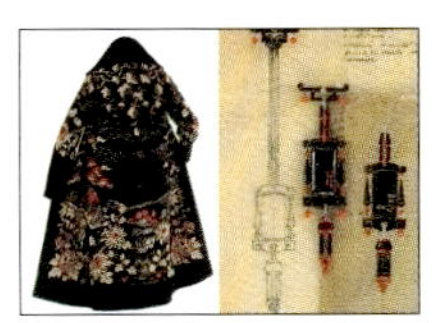

"Mandarin" evening coat by Paul Poiret, circa 1925. The couturier's art has always been intimately linked to that of the jeweler. © Richard Haughton/Kyoto Costume Institute. **"Lanterne Chinoise" pendant watch** in enamel, gold, coral and diamonds, 1924. A highlight of the Léon Hatot auction, organized by Christie's Geneva in May 1989. This watch, like many other lots in the sale, went for several times its original estimate. © Christie's Images.

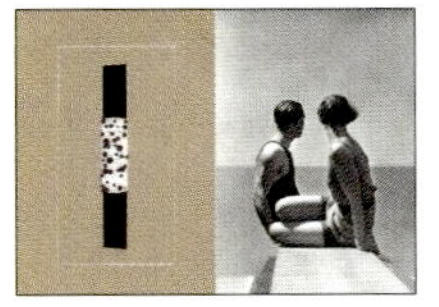

Project for a watch with a silk strap and a dial cover set with cabochon sapphires and brilliant-cut diamonds. Original drawing by Léon Hatot in pencil, ink and gouache on cardboard, circa 1925. The jeweler's legacy of sketches is an infinite source of inspiration. This drawing sparked the "Aimay" line. © Courtesy Léon Hatot Archives. **Horst P. Horst and a model** wearing Izod bathing suits, photographed by George Hoyningen-Huene, circa 1930. © Condé Nast Archive/Corbis.

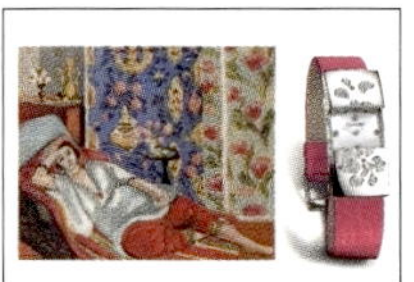

Henri Matisse, *Odalisque in Red Pants,* 1924-1925. "There are flowers everywhere if we only know how to see them." (Matisse). Jean Walter and Paul Guillaume collection, Musée de l'Orangerie, Paris. © Succession Matisse/RMN. **Watch from the contemporary "Mae" line** in white gold, diamonds, pink sapphires and mother-of-pearl with a satin strap. Each petal is fashioned from a cluster of diamonds. Inspired by Japanese art, Léon Hatot chose floral motifs for many of his creations. © Courtesy Léon Hatot Archives.

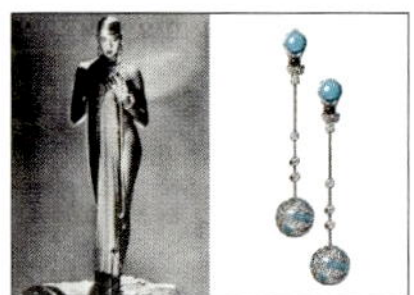

Joséphine Baker reigned over Parisian nights after 1925. This ebony goddess gave the capital its first taste of exoticism and sensuality. © Rue des Archives, Paris. **Drop earrings from the contemporary "Luela" line** in cabochon turquoises and onyx, diamonds, lacquer and white gold. Pendants in every shape and size were all the rage in the nineteen-twenties, as were drop earrings which stole the spotlight from simple studs. © Courtesy Léon Hatot Archives.

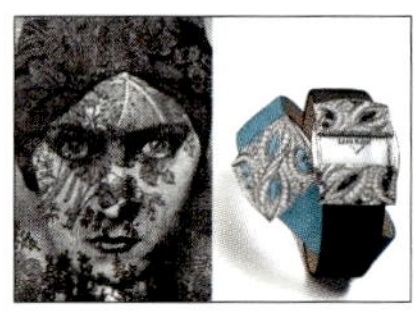

Gloria Swanson, photographed by Edward Steichen in 1924. The Museum of Modern Art, New York. © 2004, Courtesy of the Museum of Modern Art, NY/Scala, Florence. **"Luela" watches** in cabochon turquoises or onyx, diamonds, mother-of-pearl and white gold with a watered silk strap. A timepiece for the day which at a touch transforms into jewelry for the evening. Léon Hatot imagined multiple variations on this distinctive concept. © Courtesy Léon Hatot Archives.

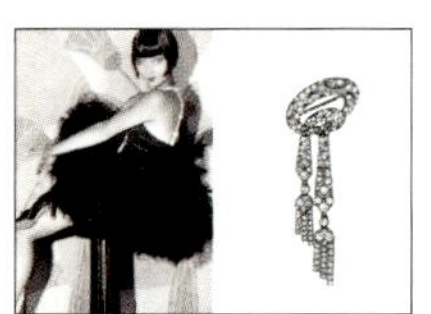

Louise Brooks, 1928. The mesmerizing silent-movie star (1906-1985), known for her trademark black bob, was the first to dance the Charleston in Europe. © Paramount/ The Kobal Collection/Richee, E.R.
Pendant brooch in diamonds and platinum, a delicate lacelike creation that has been skillfully knotted into a "scarf" whose tassels, a characteristic feature of late nineteen-twenties design, hang free. © Courtesy Léon Hatot Archives.

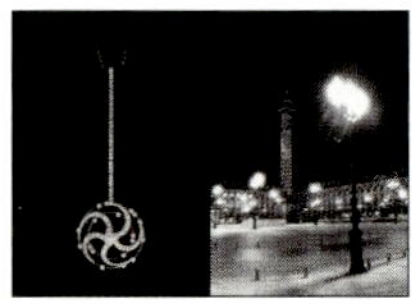

"Coup de Foudre Vertige" pendant in diamonds and white gold. The "weak at the knees" feeling that comes with love inspired the Hatot designers for this new jewelry line, with its swirling spiral motifs. © Courtesy Léon Hatot Archives.
Place Vendôme in Paris, home to the most prestigious names in fine jewelry to whom Léon Hatot, from his premises on Rue du Faubourg Saint-Honoré, lent his talent. © Assouline.

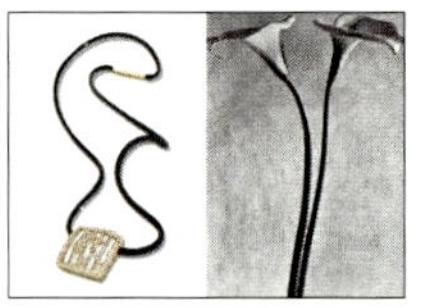

"Kimay Mystère" pendant in yellow gold, white mother-of-pearl and diamonds. Japan has captivated Western artists and craftsmen, and the sense of space and ornamentation that distinguish Japanese art are evident in the "Kimay" line. © Courtesy Léon Hatot Archives.
Tina Modotti, *Calla Lilies,* 1925. © The Detroit Institute of Arts.

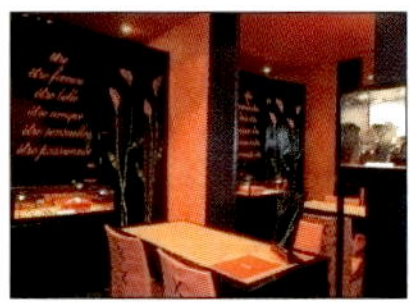

Inside the Léon Hatot boutique at 7, Rue de la Paix. The inauguration in December 2003 of the boutique, all in black and coral, marked the return to the French capital of the master jeweler's art and spirit. © Courtesy Léon Hatot Archives.

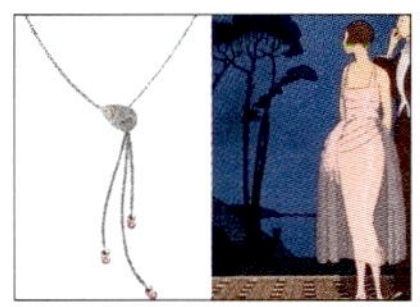

"Aimay" necklace in diamonds, cabochon and briolette pink sapphires, and white gold. The "Aimay" line is one of contrast, with the soft curves of the cabochon sapphires dialoguing with a sparkling pavé of brilliant-cut diamonds. © Courtesy Léon Hatot Archives.

"Douce nuit", illustration published in *Le Bon Ton* of an evening dress by Worth, 1920. © Gianni Dagli Orti/Corbis.

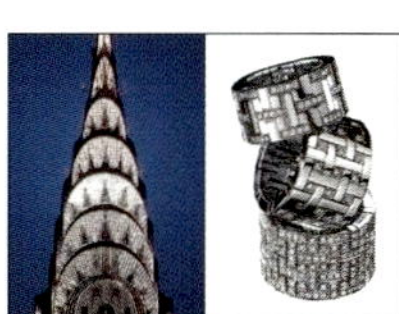

The Chrysler Building (architect William Van Alen, 1928-1930) in Manhattan is a stunning symbol of Art Deco. The building, which culminates in a steel spire, was erected for the industrial magnate Walter P. Chrysler as a tribute to the automobile. © Bo Zaunders/Corbis. "Zelia" rings in diamonds and white gold. The first and most structured of the contemporary collections, "Zelia" lends its careful geometries of precious metals and stones to innumerable interpretations. © Courtesy Léon Hatot Archives.

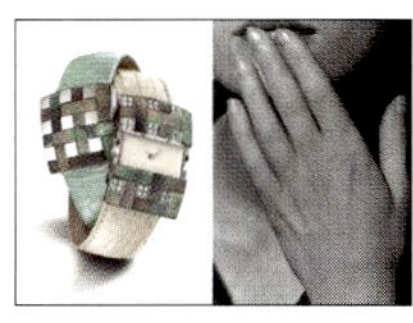

"Zelia" watches in steel, black mother-of-pearl, diamonds and lacquer with an alligator or teju strap. Steel meets mother-of-pearl for these precious cases whose interweavings are highlighted with diamonds. © Courtesy Léon Hatot Archives.

Man Ray, *No title,* 1931. © Man Ray Trust/Adagp, Paris 2005.

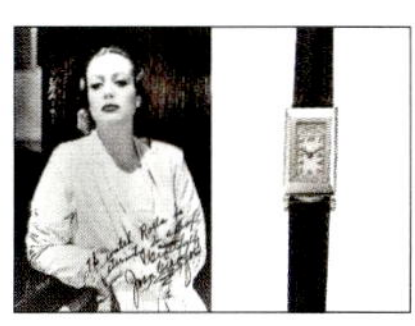

The Hollywood star Joan Crawford gave a sophisticated definition of the "Rolls" watch: "The watch Rolls is eternity in a box." The "Rolls", a revolutionary self-winding watch, was designed by the master watchmaker in 1930. The movement "rolls" back and forth on tiny ball bearings that regulate its pace. © Courtesy Léon Hatot Archives.

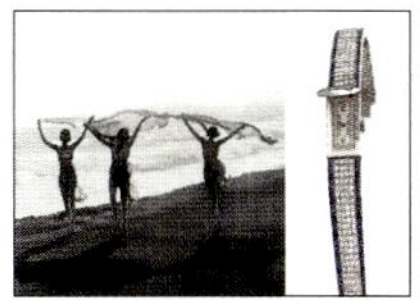

Isadora Duncan performs an improvised dance on the beach, circa 1910. Léon Hatot immortalized the movements of the barefoot dancer on cigarette cases, card holders and cufflinks. © Underwood & Underwood/Corbis. Watch in diamonds, sapphires and platinum, circa 1925. Constantly on show thanks to new sleeveless fashions, and chosen to complement evening wear, the wristwatch was in the spotlight throughout the Roaring Twenties. © Courtesy Léon Hatot Archives.

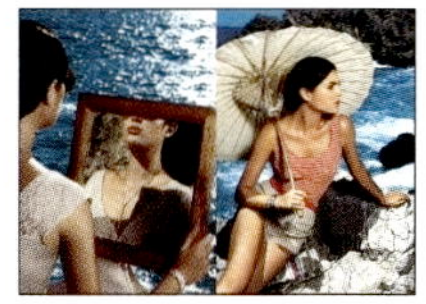

"Aimay" line: "Aimay Pampille" necklace in diamonds, cabochon pink sapphires and white gold; "Aimay Classique" watch in white gold, diamonds, cabochon pink sapphires and mother-of pearl with an alligator strap. "Kimay" and "Zelia" lines: "Kimay 4 Saisons" watch in yellow gold, diamonds, garnets and mother-of-pearl with a shagreen strap; "Zelia" ring in diamonds and yellow gold. © Paolo Zambaldi for *Vogue Gioiello*, Milano/Condé Nast.

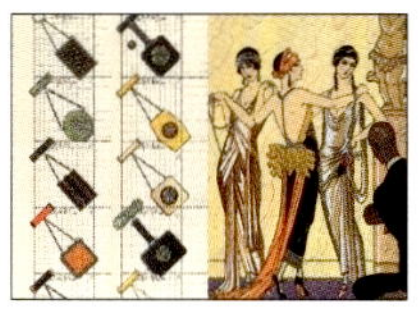

Extracts from Léon Hatot's production register, 1922-1923. The *nécessaire* was a lady's essential companion through Parisian evenings. It cleverly combined, in the least possible space, a mirror, a compact, a lipstick holder, a comb, a cigarette case and lighter, and sometimes even a miniature watch. © Courtesy Léon Hatot Archives. "The Judgment of Paris" by George Barbier, 1920s. © Stapleton Collection/Corbis.

The author wishes to thank the Hatot family and Léon Hatot master jeweler and watchmaker for their precious contribution, in particular Ariane Maradan at the company's archives for historic and artistic documents, and the marketing and public relations departments. Thank you also to Martine and Prosper Assouline, François Curiel, Chairman of Christie's Europe, Pierre Mongeau, Jean-Claude Sabrier, the library of art and archaeology (Geneva), the library of decorative arts (Paris), the national museums' central library (Paris) and the Chancellery of the Legion of Honor (Paris).